BEGIN
AGAIN,
BELIEVE
AGAIN

BEGIN AGAIN, BELIEVE AGAIN

Embracing the
Courage to Love
with Abandon

Sharon A. Hersh

ZONDERVAN.com/
AUTHORTRACKER
follow your favorite authors

ZONDERVAN

Begin Again, Believe Again
Copyright © 2010 by Sharon Hersh

This title is also available as a Zondervan ebook.
Visit www.zondervan.com/ebooks.

This title is also available in a Zondervan audio edition.
Visit www.zondervan.fm.

Requests for information should be addressed to:
Zondervan, *Grand Rapids, Michigan* 49530

Library of Congress Cataloging-in-Publication Data

Hersh, Sharon A.
    Begin again, believe again : embracing the courage to love with abandon / Sharon A.
Hersh.
        p.   cm.
    Includes bibliographical references.
    ISBN 978-0-310-31899-6 (softcover)
    1. Christian women — Religious life. 2. Interpersonal relations — Religious aspects —
Christianity. I. Title.
BV4527.H479   2010
248.8'43 — dc22   2010019075

All Scripture quotations, unless otherwise indicated, are taken from *The Message.*
Copyright © 1993, 1994, 1995, 1996, 2000, 2001, 2002. Used by permission of NavPress
Publishing Group.

Scripture quotations marked NIV are taken from the Holy Bible, *New International
Version®, NIV®.* Copyright © 1973, 1978, 1984 by Biblica, Inc.™ Used by permission of
Zondervan. All rights reserved worldwide.

Cover design: Gayle Raymer
Cover photography or illustration: Aflo
Interior design: Melissa Elenbaas

Printed in the United States of America

10 11 12 13 14 15 /DCI/ 22 21 20 19 18 17 16 15 14 13 12 11 10 9 8 7 6 5 4 3 2 1

To my children,
Kristin and Graham,
my reason and role models for
trying, risking, forgiving, hoping,
beginning and believing again.

Contents

Acknowledgments

THE BRAVERHEARTS WHO LET us into their lives by telling their stories: Annie Biers, Josh and Keely Leim, Cyndi Hart, Sara Lyons, Elaine Storck, Raeann Phillips, Rachel Stratford, Gigi Townsend, Kristin Golden, Sally Basefsky, Emily Miller, Dottie Phelps, Ann Trawick, Judy Grarock, Sarah Francois, and Amanda Pennington.

The braverhearts who let me into my own life by being a part of my story: my counselor, Tino Romero, whose faith lifted me out of myself and into a greater story; my rescuers, Elaine (you still have my house key!) and Clint and Jen Clark, who hoped for me when I could not hope for myself; my pastor, Peter Hiett (and his sweet wife, Susan), who relentlessly reminds me that God's love is deeper than our human stories; my community, who freely shares stories that allow us to love, laugh, cry, pray, dream, begin again, and believe again — Sam and Kerstin Kimbriel, Ben and Joanna Phillips, Frances and Bill Forgione, Justin and Karissa Bullis, William and Dana Brereton, Ann and Andrew Trawick, Ray and Judy Bruce, Jonathan and Angie DenHartog, Kevin and Kelli Miller, Mark LaFleur, Xan and Jayne Hood, Judy Nelson, Dave and Shari Meserve, Kristine Eives, and Tamara White.

My parents, John and Kathleen Baker, who model beginning and believing again and again and again and again.

Dudley Delffs, Senior Vice President, who inspired me to begin working with Zondervan. You were right—the professionalism and creativity of this publisher have made the work easy and exciting.

Sandy Vander Zicht and the entire editing team, including Brian Phipps: your editing advice and expertise have taught me much. Your heart for excellence has been a "north star" during the entire process.

And to all my readers: I eagerly look forward to the day when we will all be together reviewing our stories, and no one will be sad, because we will be with the One who is the beginning and ending of all our stories.

Begin Again

Aye, fight and you may die. Run and you'll live … at least a while. And dying in your beds, many years from now, would you be willin' to trade ALL the days, from this day to that, for one chance, just one chance, to come back here and tell our enemies that they may take our lives, but they'll never take … OUR FREEDOM!

—William Wallace, *Braveheart*

God has created each one of us, every human being, for greater things—to love and to be loved. But why did God make some of us men and others women? Because a woman's love is one image of the love of God, and a man's love is another image of God's love…. That special power of loving that belongs to a woman is seen most clearly when she [gives herself to others]. No job, no plans, no possessions, no idea of "freedom" can take the place of love. So anything that destroys [the capacity to love] destroys his most precious gift to women—the ability to love as a woman.

—Mother Teresa of Calcutta

WHAT IS THE FIRST thing you thought about this morning? Prayed about last night? Worried over throughout the day? I imagine if we could have a face-to-face conversation about what you think about, dream for, persistently pray about, risk for over and over again, discuss with your friends, are willing to look like a fool for, and continually hope for *more* in, we would see your heart for relationships. Our longing for relationships is at the very core of our design as women. We experience the truth that Mother Teresa expressed: no job, plans, or possessions can take the place of loving and being loved. Deep within every woman's heart is a longing for relationships. But we want more than ordinary relationships; we long for the extraordinary.

We may not immediately see the similarity between our longing for relationships and the story of the famous warrior with a brave heart, William of Wallace, yet I have come to understand that women hear "Freedom!" in the declaration that they were made for relationships. Over the past ten years, I have heard stories of women willing to fight for, risk for, be fools for, and even die to themselves for the sake of relationships. They might not wear war paint or ride off on battle horses, but I know countless bravehearts who have fought for their marriages, children, friendships, and ministries. Allow me to introduce you to one of my favorites. Her name is Annie.

When I first met Annie, she was my student in graduate school, studying to be a counselor. During a lunch break, she confessed to me that she was in a tumultuous relationship characterized by many destructive addictive patterns. She wanted out, but she was afraid of being alone. Annie wrestled with her growing understanding that she was designed with a heart for relationships but that she had distorted her design by choosing a relationship that was draining life from her. Eventually Annie accepted the invitation to trust God with her future and her loneliness, and she broke off this violent and destructive relationship. Two weeks later, she learned that she was pregnant.

Annie returned briefly to her home church where she bravely confessed her failures to her family and to the congregation, which had helped pay her graduate school tuition. Annie's mother moved to Annie's town for the final trimester of Annie's pregnancy to support her in every way possible.

As Annie's mother joined the routine of Annie's life, she noticed the practical and kind attentiveness of Annie's friend Matt. Matt was the first person Annie called with the terrible and wonderful news that she was pregnant. He immediately came over and stayed with Annie as she wept—howled, really—unable to get up off the floor. Matt helped Annie get a restraining order against her violent boyfriend. He bought groceries when Annie's refrigerator was almost empty. Annie was so busy dealing with the hard realities of her choices and the scary decisions about her future that she didn't notice God had brought a "kinsman-redeemer" into her life.[1] But Annie's braveheart mother noticed, and she gently began to nudge Annie to see the significant role that Matt was playing in her life.

Matt won Annie's heart, bought back her dignity, avenged her shame, delivered her from being a single mother, redeemed her careless and foolish choices, and rescued her and her baby boy, Joey, when he married her and adopted Joey as his own. I saw Annie and her little family not long ago and was amazed at the transformation in her life. She was full of new life and ready to tell the world that mistakes can be redeemed, that babies are worth fighting for, and that forgiveness can set you free.

Annie's braveheart story is the kind we love to read. We may wince at her brokenness, but we rejoice at her courage in offering it to God for his transforming power. However, as thrilling as their story may be, I know that Annie, Matt, and little Joey are not living a fairy-tale life. Matt sometimes gets mad about Annie's past. Annie still feels shame. And Joey keeps them up all night just being a baby. Annie is experiencing the reality that relationships, even relationships that have Hollywood endings, are hard.

I am familiar with many other painful braveheart stories, stories that include a wife learning too late of the financial irresponsibility of her scheming husband, who slowly spent all of the family's resources, and a mother finding her thirteen-year-old daughter—who only yesterday it seems was wearing pigtails—using a pocketknife to carve the hieroglyphics of her pain onto her arms and legs. Unbearable stories of infidelity in a thirty-year marriage; a baby born without a portion of her brain; a son ravaged by AIDS who is dying in a hospice, estranged from his family. You have probably heard similarly heart-wrenching stories. Maybe you are living one.

My own braveheart story began in 2001, when my husband of twenty years told me that he was lonely (I was busy writing and speaking about relationships!), that he'd found a soul mate, and that he wanted a divorce. My family broke into a million pieces that all of the counseling and wisdom in the world could not put back together again.

The divorce was just the first traumatic event in a harrowing eight-year season of difficulties for my family. I relapsed in my alcoholism, and in the process, I hurt and scared a lot of people, including me. My son got depressed and tried marijuana; he told me it gave him a little peace. Who could blame him? My daughter became a cheerleader, got straight A's, and was voted most likely to uphold the biblical values of her Christian middle school. Eight years later she told me that she thought she was an alcoholic. My best friend of over ten years told me that she wanted a different path for her life than the one I was on and could no longer remain in our friendship.

I tell you about my broken and battered heart with a bit of fear and trembling. Making one's failures public is a scary thing. Yet I know that you too have stories of heartache. The truth is we all fail. We all have relationships that falter. We all have conflicts that we don't know how to resolve. We all have children who go in a different direction than the one we dreamed for them. We all have friends who promise to be there for us and then drop out of our lives. We all get lonely.

Ask any woman over the age of thirty if her relational life has turned out as she dreamed it would, and you're almost guaranteed to hear stories of hard relationships, broken relationships, even unbearable relationships. You may hear stories of failure in relationships, of inexplicable circumstances with loved ones, of singleness well into midlife while attending countless weddings of friends, or of heartbreaking splits that separate lifelong relationships. You may hear of a dreary career in a pretzel stand at the mall or of a shameful stint in a psychiatric hospital for severe depression. You may hear of a child lost to a confusing war or of a home lost to a foreclosing bank that has no regard for all the precious memories that house held. .

Yet she will tell you that she still longs for more—for purposeful, passionate, mutual relationships, for healing in her fractured family. She wants to be chosen, to belong, to be joined to another in a wonderful marriage. She wants to believe this world is a place where relationships can make a difference. She may tell you that in the midst of life's challenging and disappointing realities, she still believes her longing for relationships is good, maybe even holy. And she is hanging on to the hope, even if only by a thread, that somehow, someway, something will happen that will make it all better.

Only for the Better

A few years ago, I spoke to a group in Alabama during a cake buffet. I think they have cake buffets only in the South, and this one was the most delightful dessert indulgence I've ever experienced. One dear woman greeted me with a wonderful Southern accent, "Oh, honey" (only Southerners call forty-eight-year-olds "honey"!), "we just loved your book *Bravehearts*. We can't wait to hear more about your life!"

"Well, a lot of things have changed in my life since I wrote that book," I hesitantly responded.

"Well, only for the better, we hope!" she responded with glee.

The theme of this book is that she was right. Things in my life have changed for the better. I know more about grace, mercy, compassion, truth, hope, and love than I ever dreamed about knowing when I wrote *Bravehearts*. When I wrote that book, I knew that I was made for relationships, and I thought that meant I knew what I wanted: human relationships. Slowly, I have discovered that most of us don't know what we really want, but God remains steadfast in his commitment to use our longing for relationships to bring us to what we most deeply want: a relationship with him. That means knowing Jesus, the One who is grace, mercy, compassion, truth, hope, and love—the One who is the plot and the meaning of all our stories of human relationships. Growing to have an intimate relationship with him is the meaning of the beginning, middle, and end of our stories.

A braverheart surrenders to the process of believing that if she had all the wisdom and power of God and could truly see the scope of her entire story, she would choose exactly the path that she has been on, because the end of that path is Jesus. You can see why that perspective requires bravery, supernatural bravery, because we naturally want good but lesser things: a kind and attentive husband, children who do their homework, and a small group at church that actually meets on a regular basis.

The Courage to Begin Again

This book tells the stories of women who have had the courage to begin again and believe again, even though their relationships have brought failure, brokenness, fractured families, addiction, abuse, judgment, and shattered dreams. These stories of braverhearts are about women who had brave dreams of creating a family, maintaining strong friendships, and knowing their purpose in life but then found things falling apart. They remind us that faith, purpose, strong values, and fierce convictions do not slay the dragons of danger and destruction in our relational worlds. In fact, God did not design us with a heart for relationships so that we could slay dragons at all. He gave us a heart for relationships because waking up every morning and beginning again, believing again, forgiving again, risking again, and dwelling in the possibilities again—that takes a real hero. A *braverheart*.

A braverheart discovers that human relationships are intended to lead us to a divine relationship. Human relationships are the path to lead us to an intimate relationship with Jesus, so that knowing him (or experiencing and feeling him) remains regardless of whether we fail or our relationships falter. The braverheart longs for a relationship with him more than it longs for the perfect marriage, the Christmas-letter children (you know, the ones who get straight A's, are elected president of the student body, and go on mission trips to Africa, where they lead hundreds to Christ!), and the friends that never fail.

Braverheart Mother Teresa of Calcutta warned, "So anything

that destroys [the capacity to love] destroys his most precious gift to women—the ability to love as a woman." We will look unflinchingly at the experiences and realities that can destroy our capacity to love and leave us bitter and resentful, enclosing our hearts in a hard protective covering, fearing that a fire-breathing dragon could appear again and painfully melt all our cherished longings, maybe even our very being.

Mother Teresa continues, "No job, no plans, no possessions, no idea of 'freedom' can take the place of love." Our brave hearts, designed for relationships, become braver hearts when we begin to desire an intimate relationship with the bravest heart, the One whose name is Love. We begin to believe that God's intention from the beginning was to give us what we really want: the Love that has been looking for us since the day we were born.

This is not a self-help book about how to make relationships work. This is a book about beginning again with a new story, a story that is deeper than our longing for human relationships, a story that unfolds in the midst of our daily and difficult relationships, a story that is redeemed as we surrender our hearts that long for relationships to the One who longs for us most.

In parts 1 and 2 of this book, we will look at beginning again and believing again in daily relationships and difficult relationships, because both are an opportunity for transformation. In part 3, we will explore how all of the painful, wonderful, difficult, and disappointing realities in relationships can redeem our desires so that we can live with deeper faith, wilder hope, and more extravagant love than we ever dreamed possible.

The good, good news is that God's most precious gift to women—the very ability to love as a woman, to take a chance again and again on love—is most beautiful when we surrender our hard relationships, our challenging relationships, and especially our unbearable relationships to the bravest heart, the One who when he sees us cries in delight, "Bone of my bones and flesh of my flesh!"; the One who is bound to us from the foundation of the world in an eternal covenant; the One who hung, stripped and naked, on the cross for the sake of a relationship with us.

Do you see what this means? Every song of longing, every romance novel of longing, every braveheart's story of longing is about him. The longing we feel—the craving we feel to be joined to another, to rest with another, to be chosen by another, to be in communion with another—it's all about him. This desire, longing, and passion is woven into the depths of our beings so that we can know, heart and soul, the love God has for us in Christ Jesus. He is our helper, our advocate, our lover, our companion, and our groom.

And the news that is oh-too-good to be true is that he longs too. He longs to come to us with healing, strength, love, and tender compassion. He longs to fill our empty craving with a relationship with himself.

Our human relationships are all a chance to surrender our brave hearts to Jesus, the bravest heart, and in so doing, we become braverhearts.

So when those dragons of danger and destruction come, begin again, and *believe*, "There is no fear in love. But perfect love drives out fear" (1 John 4:18 NIV).

PART 1

Begin Again, Believe Again
in Daily Relationships

Marriage is a taste of heaven and a taste of hell.

—Dan Allender,
Intimate Allies

Parenting is a mysterious task. First you create an intimate, all-consuming attachment with your [child], then you spend the rest of your life learning to let [her] go.

—Judy Ford,
Between Mother and Daughter

All of this waiting ... between [relationships] is the hard work, isn't it? The sweet tastes feel so few and far between. [They] do come ... in the giggle of a child, in forgiveness when we've wronged a friend, in touch at a tender moment. Even in sorrow and sadness there can be full beauty, goodness, and truth. We ache because we have loved.

—Judy Nelson, editor,
Worldwide Challenge

In part 1, we will explore the paradoxical truth that the gifts of longing, brokenness, and hope are found in the glory of our desire for relationships. In chapter 1, we will begin with a reminder that we were made for relationships. God breathed into us a holy longing for relationships that even the daily realities and disappointments of life cannot extinguish. The beautiful ache — our longing for relationships — remains through all the ups and downs of our relational lives. We will examine two different strategies women often use to respond to the beautiful ache: becoming dreamers who cling to idealism rather than face life on life's terms or becoming schemers who try to manage not only their hearts but also everyone in their lives. Both strategies confirm that even though difficulties and disappointments in relationships are inevitable, we get confused about how we should respond to the brokenness.

Chapter 2 explores the brokenness we experience in our daily relationships with family, friends, and coworkers. Even when we are not experiencing a crisis in our relationships, we still experience "paper cuts" — words or gestures that nick our hearts and hurt. When we dare to believe that disappointment and heartache are gifts, we move from being a braveheart who just longs for relationships to being a braverheart who continues to desire More even when things get pretty rough. The ache that remains after heartbreaking experiences and even in the midst of good relationships is intended to guide us to more than human relationships. The brokenness we experience when we just can't make things work out no matter how hard we try, beg, plead, manipulate, control, bribe, induce guilt, or offer ultimatums, can become the path to real rest if we can find Someone to rest in who is greater than ourselves and our human relationships. Chapter 3 tells the stories of three women who face the challenges of relationships with hope — risk-taking, life-giving, world-changing hope. Their stories remind us that all of our daily relationships—with our spouses, our aging parents, our good friends; with whining, demanding children who leave us exhausted; with rebellious, demanding teenagers who leave us afraid; or with the loneliness that comes in curling up in bed at night alone—all of these daily relationships and their inevitable challenges were intended to lead to hope that is rooted in the unshakeable truth that we are joined to Another who will never leave us or forsake us.

CHAPTER ONE

The Beautiful Ache

The soul is made of love, and must ever strive to
return to love. Therefore, it can never find rest nor
happiness in other things. It must lose itself in love.
By its very nature it must seek God, who is love.

—Mechthild of Magdeburg

SEVERAL YEARS AGO, I took the whole month of December
off from work. I had visions of cleaning out closets and spending quality time with my children. I also watched a lot of television and discovered a show that completely fascinated me.
For those of us who are domestically dysfunctional, *The Martha Stewart Show* is an amazing program. On one show, Martha made an elaborate gingerbread house that looked better
than the house I live in, and it took her only twenty minutes!

Watching Martha Stewart inspired much grander dreams
for my one-month sabbatical. Instead of cleaning closets
or playing Scrabble with the kids, I had visions of painting

sunflowers on our garbage can, growing an organic garden, and sewing elaborate outfits for my children. Maybe we could even start entertaining with theme parties. I approached my family with the idea of having our friends over for a Hawaiian night. We could decorate and cook special food and even wear Hawaiian clothes. My children, who were all too familiar with my mediocre domestic skills asked, "Why would we do this?" That Christmas they gave me a sign that I still have in my kitchen: "Martha Stewart Doesn't Live Here."

It didn't take long for me to recognize why I had attached myself to Martha. She seemed to have a foolproof formula for domestic bliss. Ever since I was a young teenager, I have been looking for a foolproof formula that would give me the deep relationships that I longed for. At various times, I have thrown myself into doing what everyone else was doing to win friends, into academic achievement to gain affirmation, and into overinvolvement with church activities to win the respect of others. Although I haven't always been able to put words to it, I have always known that my deepest longing—what drove my involvement in these activities—was for intimate and lasting relationships.

If it were possible for you to peel back all the layers of your longings, I have no doubt you would discover a desire for rich, deep, fulfilling relationships—a desire so intense that even the inevitable relational failures and disappointments can't extinguish it.

Our longings to be chosen, joined to another, have babies, keep our families from danger, unify our families around common values and goals (like Hawaiian dinner parties!), live with purpose, heal our wounds, make a difference, survive loss, and give and receive forgiveness are not random characteristics. These longings and attributes are part of how God designed us uniquely as women. In God's first story about men and women, we learn that he formed Eve from Adam's side. Eve was born into a relationship. Humanly speaking, she was never alone. Her attachment to the relational was more conscious and more compelling than Adam's. God had to tell Adam, "It's not good for the Man to be alone" (Gen. 2:18). From the beginning, women were designed to be dependent on the ability to enjoy warm attachments, close relationships, and interdependent bonding.

In every woman there is an inner tug, an ache that propels us toward relationships. You may have felt it on your first day in school when you surveyed all of the other girls and wondered how you could belong. Maybe you felt it last week after you had a meaningful conversation with your husband that you wished didn't have to end. I feel it every time I look at pictures of my grown children and think about how I miss them and all that I long for them to experience. I felt it at church a few weeks ago during our extended worship time after our service, a time of praying, singing, and meditating. This particular Sunday, I moved to the front of the sanctuary and sank down in my chair. I needed something. As the lights dimmed and the band played, I got a sense that I was the only one in the sanctuary. I couldn't see anyone sitting around me. And there in the dark, with the music flooding my heart and soul, I cried out to God, "I need you."

God designed us with this beautiful ache to lead us into a life of love. When we believe that our longing for relationships is about only human relationships, we get frustrated, because human relationships often fall short. When we become determined to satiate or soothe our longings with people-pleasing, alcohol, work, food, perfectionism, among other things, we get confused about where God intends our longings ultimately to take us. We mistakenly believe that the ache is calling us to something merely external. What we seek is always just around the corner, and when we reach the corner, it has ducked out of sight. Yet our longing for relationships is so strong that even after turning the corner a thousand times, we still say, "*This* is going to be the relationship, the formula, the experience that works—that satisfies me." Life becomes an endless pilgrimage around corners.

The soul is a pilgrim.

—John Ruysbroeck,
The Adornment of a Spiritual Marriage

The beautiful ache can be frustrating and confusing. That's why we come up with strategies to manage our longings in hopes that we can figure out a way to get what we want. The two strategies I have experienced and seen most often in the lives of other women are *dreaming* and *scheming*. We may begin as a dreamer, hoping that all of these longings will result in a "happily ever after" story. When we start to realize that our dreams might not come true, we find another strategy and become schemers. A schemer is determined to take matters into her own hands and have some sense of control. Both the dreamer and the schemer are energized by the belief that our longings were intended to send us in a mad pursuit of what we want. It is humbling and a little scary to realize that God uses our longings, our shattered dreams, and our foolish schemes to reveal what we most deeply want: a relationship with him.

The Dreamer

When I was in college, I sang this little song:

> I'm tired of college life
> I want to be somebody's wife
> I'd rather do dishes for somebody's kisses
> I'm tired of college life

Like most young women of my generation, I dreamed of

marriage, family, and a beautiful home with a white picket fence to satisfy all my longings. The ideal life beckoned me with promises of perfect peace and endless bliss. I was a dreamer. A dreamer wants the ideal. She is drawn to the promise of romance, well-behaved children, and the lifestyles of the rich and famous. But being a dreamer has a dark side. When dreams become agendas, the only right way to do things, or the proof that we are good, no room is left for family and friends to have their own dreams, make mistakes, or try new things. Shattered dreams bring shame rather than trust that God brings beauty from ashes.

After speaking at a parenting conference a few years ago, a dear older woman approached me with tears streaming down her face. She described how her dreams for her children had poisoned her mothering, and she expressed deep regret for her idealistic and unrealistic parenting. "I expected my son to be a certain way, no matter what," she explained. "I crushed his individuality and drove him away from me." This mother's dreams weren't necessarily wrong, but her response when she was disappointed kept her from offering life to her relationships.

> *The ideal may actually lull us into ruin.*
>
> —Oswald Chambers,
> *My Utmost for His Highest*

Dreams and Disappointments

The dark side of dreaming shows itself when we don't know what to do with disappointment. When Sam and Liza got married, they immediately began to dream about creating a family. They both wanted to pursue an international adoption. After a few years of marriage, they traveled to Ethiopia to get their beautiful baby girl, Selah. They had faced struggles with family members who didn't understand why they wanted to adopt, with the financial and legal hurdles of adoption, and with fears of the unknown about their future child. They were ready for this dream to come true.

Sam and Liza dreamed what they believed was God's dream for their lives and bravely followed that dream. They knew Selah had experienced extreme malnutrition and would have some health complications. What they didn't know is that the complications would eventually lead doctors to conclude that beautiful little Selah might never speak. When Sam and Liza began the adoption process, they had no way to anticipate all of the disappointments they would experience along the way. They have never been disappointed in Selah, but mounting medical bills, impending surgeries, endless hours of caring for a very sick little girl, and agonizing questions about suffering are the excruciating realities that they have had to face. Perhaps you can identify with Liza. She dreamed good dreams. Unselfish dreams. Godly dreams. Maybe you have channeled your longing for relationships in wonderful ways—loving a difficult spouse, raising children with special needs or rebellious hearts, caring for aging parents, offering out of your singleness to motherless or fatherless children—only to be met with disappointment and more difficulties. We tend to believe that if we dream God's dreams, then surely he will give us all the desires of our hearts. But we are often disappointed.

Dreams and Donkeys

I couldn't help but think about this confusion over God's dreams and our dreams when I was in Israel a few years ago. It was incredible, standing at the top of the Mount of Olives, looking down over the beautiful, lush Kidron Valley and gazing across to the other side, the city of Jerusalem. I was deeply moved as I listened to my pastor read the gospel texts of Jesus' triumphal entry into the city, the event we now commemorate as Palm Sunday. This setting, so rich with history, and the New Testament story my pastor read made me think about how easy it is to get confused about our dreams and God's dreams.

I stood there and tried to imagine what it might have been like on that day over two thousand years ago. As we slowly walked down a narrow road into Jerusalem, I envisioned the royal processional that everyone must have been expecting for the messianic King, the son of David, entering the city. It wasn't hard to imagine that the celebratory crowd might have been confused and disappointed with what they saw instead: Jesus riding a lowly donkey.

How many people that day were surprised, upset, and disappointed that their leader, their King, couldn't do better than a donkey? They believed the Messiah would deliver them from Roman occupation and oppression and restore the kingdom of David to its glory. They wanted a hero, and they probably wanted him to look like a hero. Jesus' triumphal entry into Jerusalem was an opportunity to show strength, to exhibit royal status, to make a statement, and to show people what his kingship would look like—a time to make everyone's dreams come true.

But Jesus confused them and confounded their expectations and dreams. He entered the city on a beast of burden, not a beast of war. He chose to ride among them on an animal of the common folk: a gentle, humble, dependable donkey. I suspect that the crowds were looking for something more, maybe a beautiful, high-stepping thoroughbred. For some folks, Christ's entry on a donkey must have felt like a shattered dream.

Pastor and theologian Dan Clendenin writes, "Jesus' 'triumphal entry' into the clogged streets of Jerusalem was a deeply ironic, highly symbolic, and deliberately provocative act. It dramatized his subversive mission and message.... Identifying with Jesus and patterning our lives after him results in endless subversions."[1] In the act of riding on a donkey, Jesus subverted the narrow political dreams of his followers in order to fulfill God's larger dream of redemption. It was an act that signaled a divine truth: Jesus had come not to conquer a government but to conquer the human heart. And his subversive work didn't stop with his earthly ministry; it continues, endlessly, in the lives of all who follow him.

This confusing and mysterious mission of Jesus became very personal for me during a Sunday morning church service years ago. It was Valentine's Day, a good day to ruminate (and even obsess) about the many painful, disappointing relationships in my life. The pastor ended his sermon by summing up the purpose of suffering in our lives: "Can you hear the tender whisper of Jesus [in the midst of your disappointment]: 'All of this was allowed, orchestrated, and done to conquer you?'" I longed to believe that dreams and disappointments, donkeys and humiliating circumstances, as well as broken and healing relationships were about conquering my heart so that God could love me more fully and I could be more fully in love with him, but it was a hard idea to hold on to when so many of my relationships seemed threatened.

It is a leap of faith to believe that having our dreams subverted is sometimes a necessary part of the pilgrimage to find our heart's true desire. The dictionary defines *subversion* as "an activity that undermines, destabilizes, or topples." As women, we certainly understand the subversion in our relational lives: the experiences that undermine, destabilize, and topple our dreams of intimate connection. Just like the people who lined the streets when Jesus rode in on a donkey did not see what they expected, you may think that your relational life is full of big mistakes; it is not the life you dreamed of. Then again, perhaps you are exactly where God wants you to be. It is good, though often hard, to remember that when our dreams are subverted, God is at work to conquer our hearts.

Dreams and Discontent

After I got married, it didn't take long for my little college song about marriage to topple and change:

> I'm tired of married life
> I want to be more than a wife
> I do all the dishes ... and get paid with kisses
> I'm tired of married life

When I discovered that my deepest longings could not be completely fulfilled by my spouse, I dreamed of children. And anyone who has children knows that it doesn't take too many weeks of mothering to discover that babies take more than they give, and they too leave us restless and discontent. So I jumped into ministry. And I did it all: children's church and choir, women's ministry, and even helping head the new building committee. Once again, it didn't take too many weeks of working in ministry to discover that it couldn't meet all of my longings.

Whether it's marriage, building a career, raising a family, or ministering to others—none of these have enough soul food to satisfy anyone completely. It's at this point that many of us get into trouble with addictions and other destructive behavior, trying to satisfy longings that our less-than-ideal relationships only intensify.

If you are a dreamer, I suspect you know that desire— the longing for more—in your relational life is always there. One friend portrayed it this way: "It pops up here, then over there—kind of like a gopher in an empty field!" In her book about feminine desire, author Carol Lee Flinders describes this ache as a "stubbornly recurrent itch that makes ordinary life impossible."[2]

When we cling to the ideal in relationships, we are devastated when we can't find a program or formula that makes everything work. And then what happens? What happens when we sin and fail, when our dreams topple and shatter, and when relationships falter? Here's how Liza describes her response to some of the shattered dreams in their adoption process: "I don't remember when I began to hate God in my heart. Or why I even do. His blessings abound in my life. And yet the sorrows that I have walked and that I walk now tempt me to despair."[3]

Reflect for a few minutes on some of your dreams—for your family, your friendships, your ministry. What happened when you started to realize that all your dreams weren't going to come true? Did you dismiss your dreams as stupid? Did you blame others for the disappointment? Were you mad at God? The dreamer often begins with a good plan, wonderful ideals, and honorable desires, but the dark side of dreaming comes out when disappointment invades and causes us to question ourselves, others, and God. Shattered dreams leave us feeling vulnerable and out of control. That's why the next strategy makes so much sense. It doesn't take many disappointments for us to move from dreaming to scheming.

The Schemer

The schemer lives to take control of people and situations. She plans what she will say in order to get a desired response. She often manipulates situations to control the outcome. She knows what is best and is determined to make it happen. At the first hint of losing control, the schemer scrambles to manage herself and others. A schemer often lives with a profound sense of loneliness, because it is impossible to get close to someone who is always in control.

Scheming and being in control often make sense to us, because we really do believe that we know what is best. The energy of the scheming heart is always rooted in the question, "Why doesn't God give me what I want, especially when what I'm asking is what he made me for?" That's a good question.

Perhaps you find yourself asking that question. You may be single and wondering why God would create you with a desire to be married and not bring anyone into your life. Maybe you are married and struggling with a distant or even demeaning spouse. Why would God create you to be joined to a tender, strong man and not change your husband? Perhaps you are a mother and you've poured your best into your children only to see them reject you or your values, or both, and your heart is broken. Why would God give you a mother's heart and let it break into a million little pieces?

I am not wise enough to answer these questions, but I believe that God knows the exact context in which each of us is most likely to surrender to an intimate relationship with him, and that is his deepest commitment to each of us. Perhaps that makes you angry; you don't want your dreams to be subverted by God's dream. If that's the case, you might relate to the woman who told me that she had finally made peace with some of the difficulties in her life; then while she and her husband were on a trip to celebrate their thirtieth wedding anniversary, he dropped dead of a heart attack. She said, "If this is God's context for me to know him more intimately, no thank you."

Liza had feelings similar to those of this struggling widow, feelings that propelled her into action.

I find myself furiously ignoring God and shrieking through my silence, "You are not enough. Your way is not working for me. I will assume control of my life." So I frantically make phone calls to every doctor in town and drag Selah to specialists across the country. I come up with brilliant ideas for Sam's employment and usurp his ability to find a job for himself. The problem with my bitter attempts to control is that they do not make me feel better, and I'm not sure that they make my situation better. But I do not say that with certainty, because I'm too blinded by the temptation that I could be in control to even admit that it fails me desperately every time.[4]

I can identify with the honest confessions of these two women. When our hearts are made for relationships, how do we live in a world we can't control? Our yearning for relationships isn't a mistake and it isn't wrong. What happens is that we wrongly interpret our longing, believing that we can slake our thirst with merely a drink of human relationships. Our longing for relationships was intended to lead us into a life of love. Our longings are like a spiritual code that gets scrambled by the difficulties and disappointments in life. When we use only human relationships to decipher our longings, we'll end up frustrated, confused, and even in despair. Instead, we need a decoder for the beautiful ache that remains constant and unchanging in the midst of relationships that come and go.

Decoding the Beautiful Ache

Every code has a key for unlocking its true meaning. When it comes to decoding the beautiful ache—our longing for relationships—that key consists of three things: honesty, openness, and willingness. It takes a lifetime to live and love well with the beautiful ache, but these three keys are easy to remember with the acronym HOW.

Honesty

In seeking to decipher the true meaning of the beautiful ache, we must begin by being honest about our desire. Our longing for relationships is a holy longing and is nothing to be ashamed of. I love what Origen, one of the early church fathers, writes about this yearning: "Because it is God that has sowed this seed in us, pressed it in, begotten it, it cannot be extirpated or die out; it glows and sparkles, burning and giving light, and always it moves upward toward God."[5]

Can you be honest about your longing for relationships? Even if your longing doesn't seem to "glow and sparkle" but instead seems to burn and hurt, confessing your desire for relationships—knowing that God has woven it into the fabric of your being—allows you to hold your head up and live in the light regarding your heart's desire.

When you are tempted to say, "I don't care anymore," or, "I don't need anyone," you are at risk of sending this God-breathed longing underground, which will result in a hard heart. When our longings go underground, we can't be vulnerable, express need, care authentically for others, or depend on God. When we suppress our holy, God-given longings, we slowly become less human. We either live in a robotic, depressed state or displace our longings with an addictive attachment to a person, place, or thing. Either way, we are trapped in an agonizing cycle of trying to kill our desire. Desire is the fuel of relationships. When we determine not to want or need, we shut down our longings. Killing desire has spiritual consequences. It

> *Acts of human mistrust and wrongdoing and lying accumulate, as people try to put a shroud over truth.*
>
> —Romans 1:18

is impossible to shut down desire for human relationships without shutting down desire for God.

Openness

Openness enables us to acknowledge the difficulties and disappointment we have experienced in relationships. This takes a lot of courage. When Liza first confessed her agony, her peers quickly surrounded her to prop her up with words of affirmation: "But you have been so sacrificial," and, "You saved Selah's life." Although their words were certainly true and perhaps well-intentioned, they were not life-giving because they failed to acknowledge Liza's pain and confusion. When Liza confessed her hurt and anger, she bravely chose to be vulnerable and not live behind a mask of platitudes.

A mask is anything that hides or distorts the truth about how you really feel. If you've ever worn a mask, you know that it's an excruciating and exhausting experience. Although a mask can hide a person completely, the good news is that it can also be removed. Taking off the mask that keeps us hidden from our true selves, from others, and from God will set us on the healing path to becoming a braverheart.

Openness leads to connection, and we discover that we are not alone. As we walk openly alongside others, we learn that relationships are not the destination; they are the path that leads us to something more, to an intimate relationship with Christ. When we acknowledge our desire for relationships and the way that our desire has been battered and broken, we invite God to lead us to our heart's deepest desire.

Willingness

Being honest and open about our relational life leads us to a willingness to let go of long-held dreams or schemes. When Liza confessed her desire and disappointment, she was able to surrender her need to control and could then pray, "Oh, for the freedom to trust him more fully than I trust the lie that I could do a better job than God!"[6] Surrendering our dreams and schemes allows us to accept what is. As I relax and accept what is happening in my relational life, I am able to see more clearly. Clarity comes only from a place of peace, not in the midst of anxiety. Willingness allows me to change directions, solicit new ideas, put plans on hold, or start over completely.

Are you willing to consider that the ups and downs of your relational life are intended to lead you to the more that is Christ? Can you offer a prayer of willingness to accept what is going on in your relationships and confess your designs (dreams and/or scheming) for living with them?

It is hard to let go of believing that our longing for relationships is about only human realities. Our flesh-and-blood relationships seem pretty real. We experience very real pain and joy in our relationships, so it is easy to forget that they are merely signs foreshadowing the substance of what we were really made for.

> *All those things are mere shadows cast before what was to come; the substance is Christ.*
>
> —Colossians 2:17

Echoes of More

When I was first pregnant with my daughter, Kristin, my husband and I experienced a scare when I no longer felt her moving. The doctor called for an ultrasound, and we were soon relieved to discover that everything was fine. As I lay in the doctor's office and gazed at the shadowy image on the monitor, I was in awe and wonderment at who I saw. I could not believe that this living, breathing human being with fingernails was growing inside of me! If I understand it right, an ultrasound is a fancy echo. When its sonic waves hit something solid, something real, they are reflected back to a sensor that creates the image we see on the screen.

Our experiences in human relationships are like an ultrasound echo. They often hit and reflect something real: our longing to be loved when we are good for nothing and to love another for the pure joy of love. Relationships, no matter how wonderful or painful, are echoes returning to us from the solid, true, and beautiful things God intends for us to experience in relationship with him. He is the more we're looking for.

When you are lonely, are you willing to believe that your loneliness is intended to remind you of a lonely God who wanders through the garden asking, "Where are you?"

When you are in the midst of good relationships, can you remember that they are echoes intended to make you long for the more that is found in Jesus?

When you feel shame because of your failure in relationships, will you let it lead you to the One who allows failure, not so that you can hide but so that he can be your covering?

When all of the yearnings and desires for relationship rise up within you, are you willing to let those longings lead you to the Author of desire?

When we miss all that we long for in relationships, the beautiful ache that we feel comes from the hands of a Designer who longs for relationship with us more than we can possibly imagine. He is committed to relationship with us above everything else. His entire story is about his design for a relationship with us. *This is the original purpose of our life.* The beautiful ache is an echo of a relationship that God is forming with us in the midst of our human relational difficulties.

How sad it would have been if I had held on to the picture of Kristin's ultrasound and treated it as if it were the real thing. I could have gone on and on about this incredible picture and been satisfied with it. When the labor pains came, I could have refused to go the hospital because I already had the picture. That, of course, would have been ridiculous, because once Kristin came into the world, I didn't even think about the picture.

Relationships are like that ultrasound; they are designed to nurture our longing for more, the divine and sacred more that is found only in a growing, intimate relationship with Jesus. Longings can, after all, make us cherish even more the object of our longing when it arrives. That was certainly true for me with the ultrasound and Kristin. In fact, those who are in difficult relationships just might long for a divine relationship more than those of us who stop along the way and are satisfied with the spiritual equivalent of an ultrasound picture: mere human relationships. The One we long for is Jesus. Human relationships were intended to encourage us to nurture our deepest longing for him; they are merely an echo of what is to come.

Just for You

1. Our longings often elude us. Sometimes it feels like what we seek is always just around the corner, and when we reach the corner, it has ducked out of sight. What are some of the corners you have reached in your relational life? In other words, what relationships or experiences did you believe would satisfy, only to discover that you were still restless and discontent?

2. How have your idealistic dreams for relationships impacted your relationships?

3. What schemes have you tried in your efforts to make your relationships work?

4. What mask have you constructed to cover shattered dreams and failed schemes? Draw a picture or construct a mask that represents how you have hidden parts of your story with:

- A happy face
- Anger
- Victimization
- Spiritual piety
- Defiance toward God
- Busyness

5. Reflect on a disappointment you've experienced in a relationship, and then reread the section in this chapter on HOW: Honesty, Openness, and Willingness.

   - Write an honest account of your dreams for this relationship and how they have been disappointed or how you have schemed to take control of the situation.
   - Consider opening up with a friend or two about your struggles. Ask them to pray with you and for you.
   - After reflection and prayer, consider what you are willing to do in response to this relationship. For example, are you willing to let go, try again, or seek counsel?

CHAPTER TWO

The Gift of Brokenness

Every long-lost dream led me to where you are ...
This much I know is true
That God blessed the broken road
That led me straight to you

—Rascal Flatts,
"Bless the Broken Road"

I SLIPPED INTO THE ROOM, hoping to go unnoticed. I quickly surveyed everyone in the room and felt relief that I didn't know anyone. I needed to be there, and yet at the same time I really didn't want to be. I felt a mixture of anticipation that I might get some help and anger that I was in this place again. I had promised my friends that I would attend this gathering, be honest about my struggles, and seek support. They knew that I was at a breaking point—again. I thought about the confession that I was about to make to a room full of strangers. I was lonely and exhausted. I was juggling many wonderful and

difficult relationships. I felt needy—in need of companionship, understanding, and the strength to go on. I knew that I
was vulnerable to my addictions to alcohol, working too much,
and trying to hold it all together to look good.

A question from another woman attending the meeting
jarred me out of my thoughts. "Are you Sharon Hersh?" she
asked. I sank even lower in my seat. How did she know me? I
didn't want to be recognized. I don't think I even answered. I
looked at her like a deer caught in the headlights. "I've heard
you speak at my church," she continued, "and I've read your
books." I'm not sure what else she said or what I said. I probably mumbled some response before I blurted out, "Today I'm
just Sharon—a lonely, needy, insecure, middle-aged, alcoholic woman." She kindly put her hand on my shoulder and
gave the perfect response, "Aren't we all?" and then she went
and found her seat.

I was attending an Alcoholics Anonymous meeting in a
town where I was traveling. I had been traveling a lot, working long hours, and trying to keep it all together—by myself.
All of my life I have struggled with wanting to look good,
hiding my needs, and crashing in my self-reliance. I identify
with the confession of Henri Nouwen, "I came to see that I
lived most of my life as a tightrope artist trying to walk on a
high, thin cable from one tower to the other, always waiting
for the applause when I had not fallen off and broken my leg."[1]
Despite crashing more than once, I didn't—and still don't—
surrender easily. You would think that a broken heart, broken relationships, and broken dreams would keep me on my
knees, but they don't. I am learning that to stay on that path
of surrender, it is essential for me to continue to embrace the
brokenness of living in this fallen world.

In the previous chapter, we looked at our God-given
desire for relationships and some of our dreams and schemes

for making our lives work. There is no doubt that shattered dreams, disappointments, and discontentment can leave us feeling pretty broken. When we resort to scheming by trying to keep it all together, putting band-aids on the wounds of relationships, and presenting a good front, we inevitably end up frustrated and exhausted, but for some of us, these are the only ways that we know how to be in relationships. How we long for rest! All this brokenness and the ache that remains become the unlikely context for rest if—and that's a big *if*—we can learn to surrender.

Surrender: The Three Gifts of Brokenness

Brokenness is a gift that awes us—when it is given to someone else. But when the gift of brokenness is given to us, it inspires anything but awe. It confuses us with pain and outrage, and it often leaves us ashamed that this is our gift when we imagine that everyone else is opening something much more bright and shiny. The surrendered life is possible only when we accept and embrace the gift hidden in the brokenness of our relationships.

This brokenness often comes wrapped in one of three different packages: personal failure, relational failure, or spiritual failure. How do we accept and surrender when we are in the midst of overwhelming sin, woundedness, or confusion? I've come to understand surrender as "making an exchange." Making an exchange means letting go of one idea, behavior, or commitment and replacing it with another. For example, when we experience personal brokenness, we can exchange hiding for being known. When we are in the midst of relational brokenness, we can exchange unrealistic agendas for humble messiness. And even when we feel spiritually broken, we can exchange our frustrating and exhausting ways of making life "work" for a relationship with the One who is the way, the truth, and the life (see John 14:6).

The Gift of Personal Failure

Personal failure can include sin, harm that we do to others, and neglect (or abandonment) of our values and beliefs. For women, however, personal failure is often felt when we fall short of all of the expectations that we have for ourselves and that our culture places on us. This was highlighted for me a few years ago when I spoke to a gathering of about six hundred young women, ages eighteen to twenty-one. I introduced myself by painting what I thought was an obviously unrealistic picture.

I've been married for twenty years and have a wonderful marriage. My husband cooks, cleans, and always brings me wonderful gifts. We have two children, and that's another happy story. They are healthy, do well in school, and would rather spend time with us than with anyone else! They do chores around the house just for the fun of it, although we have a house that is practically self-cleaning. We even won "Yard of the Month" twice last year. We don't need to worry about finances because we have lots of money. We buy everything that we want, and everything turns out to be exactly what we wanted. We took a vacation last year and enjoyed every minute of it, but we were glad to come home because we have jobs that we love. I'm a counselor and all of my clients are doing so well, but they keep coming back and paying me just because they like counseling! I must say that I am really happy with the way that I look too. I love my hair, my body, my wardrobe. All in all, life is just perfect!

The young women in the audience oohed and aahed. They thought I was telling the truth! I almost walked off the platform because I knew that to tell the true story would be to announce that I had failed. My marriage was breaking apart, and my children were suffering in the midst of the brokenness. Our yard had never been nominated for "Yard of the Month," and our budget was so stressed we couldn't even afford to water the lawn! That year, two dear clients had died from cancer, and I wasn't sure I could bear the pain of living in a world where you love people and then lose them. I was depressed, had

> *For all ... fall short of the glory of God.*
>
> —Romans 3:23 NIV

gained a few pounds, and everything in my wardrobe looked like it had been purchased in the previous decade! No wonder I wanted to run from the auditorium and hide. My life had fallen way short.

The Exchange: Hiding for Being Known

Personal failure can keep us from the path of surrender when we become determined to hide from others. Hiding keeps us alone and consumed with the job of hiding. I am blessed to be an alcoholic. Yes, you read that right. I'm blessed because I know that there is a place I can go, virtually anywhere in the world, where I can come out of hiding and confess my failure, my vulnerability, and my need. Many times I have begun my day by attending a meeting and making this statement: "My name is Sharon, and I'm an alcoholic." For me, that is code for the deeper reality that I am a woman in need—in need of grace, support, the strength of others, and the strength of God.

I became friends with Cyndi, the woman who approached me in the Alcoholics Anonymous meeting I described at the beginning of the chapter. Cyndi grew up in a home filled with the brokenness of addiction. As she entered adolescence, she believed the only path for her was to stay stuck in that brokenness. By the time she was thirty, Cyndi was a drug addict and an alcoholic. She had accumulated legal consequences as well as many broken relationships. After the failure of yet another relationship, Cyndi looked at her empty apartment and fell to the floor in despair. She didn't have enough money to buy any more drugs or alcohol. She contemplated suicide, but didn't even know how to do that. Then a foreign thought flitted through her mind and heart: "I could ask for help." In other words, she could exchange hiding in the prison of her addiction for being known by others who might offer her another way to live.

Cyndi had never asked for help before. Her family certainly had not modeled asking for help, but Cyndi was desperate—desperately broken. She found a telephone book and called the number of a local inpatient treatment facility and checked in the next day. As Cyndi's mind cleared and she began to learn about addiction and the path of recovery, the brokenness of her life became more apparent. She had no real friends, no vision for her future, and no hope that she could leave treatment and live differently. Cyndi's cousin came to see her while she was in treatment. She didn't know this cousin very well, but she was grateful for a visitor. Cindy's cousin left her a Bible and suggested that she read it. Cyndi told me, "I had no intention of reading it, but in the middle of the night, I felt so desperately lonely and afraid, I read it. I began to think there might be something there that I wanted." When Cyndi left treatment, she started listening to Christian radio. Although she had never listened to religious programs, her desperation kept her tuning in. She found a church through one of the radio programs, and her faith began to flourish. That was more than five years ago. Cyndi summarizes the gift of brokenness in her life better than I could: "Only complete desperation would make a crack-addict alcoholic seek

treatment, read a Bible, listen to Christian music, and want—
really want—God."

Maybe you smile at Cyndi's story and rejoice in her dramatic
conversion, wondering what it has to do with you. Spend a few
minutes thinking about your own brokenness. It may not be as
dramatic as Cyndi's, but I know that it cuts you to the core just
the same. It leaves you feeling lonely, empty, and maybe even a
little desperate for more. Sometimes our brokenness is evident
in the mundane, daily realities of our relationships. When we
yell at our children, tell a "little white lie" to our husbands
about how much we spent at the mall, or secretly resent our
friends because they seem to have it all together, we are at risk
of ending up in bondage that is just as debilitating as Cyndi's.
If we believe that we can't tell anyone we have a temper, if we
can't talk about financial realities with our husband, or if we
feel inferior to other women, we hide the very parts of us that
are most in need of compassion and companionship. Making
the exchange of hiding for being known in these realities is just
as important for us as it was for my addict-friend Cyndi.

I experienced the desperate longing to hide from others
shortly after my son was born. It didn't take long for me to
know I needed a break from two children under the age of
two! My heart was broken because I was yelling at my toddler daughter. I felt ugly and fat and didn't think that I was
doing anything well. I made the mistake of thinking a trip to
the gym was just what I needed. I pulled on my old spandex
workout clothes (whoever thought spandex was flattering?)
and tried to ignore the different bulging parts of my body. I
entered a room filled with women who looked much more fit
and together than I did. I quickly found a place in the back
row and tried to coordinate my movements to the music. At
one point, as I reached my arms into the air, I looked at myself
in the mirror at the front of the room. I looked ridiculous!

And it was quickly apparent that, unlike the other "together" women in the room, I had not shaved under my arms since before my son was born! I was mortified. I ran from the room, grabbed my stuff from the locker, and went and sat in my car and cried. I didn't ever want to face anyone again. That's what brokenness can do; it can keep us stuck in our shame, our failures, *ourselves*—our broken selves. Personal failure becomes a gift when we reach the point that Cyndi did: knowing that we need help and being willing to seek it wherever and however we can.

> *He heals the heartbroken and bandages their wounds.*
>
> —Psalm 147:3

What Are You Hiding?

Personal failure can allow you to make peace with yourself. That doesn't mean you resign yourself to a pattern of living that is deadening or destructive; it means you stop hiding the parts of you that need help, support, love, and kindness. For many years, I hid the lonely, insecure, needy, vulnerable part of me in the dark basement of my life. The postpregnancy incident at the gym further pressured me to be vigilant to present only a put-together self to the world. I was ashamed of the part of me that was broken, annoyed by her, and I just wanted her to go away. I denied her the support and kindness that she needed.

What part of yourself do you keep locked in the dark basement of your life? When you are struggling, doubting your faith, or losing hope, who do you call? When you are in need, who do you reach out to? When you feel vulnerable and insecure, who knows? When we keep those parts of ourselves locked away, we are at risk of living divided lives and becoming filled with self-hatred. When we hide our brokenness, we deny it the redemptive, healing touch that God intended for us to receive from this gift of brokenness. In his wonderful book *The Gift of Being Yourself*, David Benner writes about the healing that can come when we exchange hiding for being known: "Christian spirituality involves acknowledging all our part-selves, exposing them to God's love and letting him weave them into the new person he is making. To do this, we must be willing to welcome these ignored parts as full members of the family of self, giving them space at the family table and slowly allowing them to be softened and healed by love and integrated into the whole person we are becoming."[2]

What parts of yourself can you invite to healing grace and love? Perhaps you can begin by acknowledging the parts that you have been ashamed of or hated. Maybe you did something when you were a teenager that you have hidden or maybe you struggle with something today that you are sure no one could handle. Healing begins when we acknowledge where we are broken and confess it to God. He, of course, knows what we're hiding, but confession opens the door to a connection that allows us to experience his healing love.

An Invitation to Come out of Hiding

So how do you come out of hiding? You might start by writing a letter to the part of yourself that you have left locked in the basement. Invite her out of hiding, apologize for how you've treated her, and acknowledge the gifts she brings to your life. This exchange will place you on the path of surrender. After the Alcoholics Anonymous meeting where I met Cyndi, I wrote the following letter to myself.

Dear broken, lonely, insecure, needy Sharon,

Without you, I wouldn't need Jesus — I mean really need him.

Without you, I wouldn't have a chance to believe that I am loved for who I am, not for what I do.

Without you, I wouldn't need a message of grace and mercy.

Without you, I wouldn't experience the care and concern of my friends.

Without you, the blood of Christ, which cleanses from every sin, would not be so meaningful.

Without you, I wouldn't be in Alcoholics Anonymous and know the many wonderful people who meet in those rooms.

Without you, the presence of the Holy Spirit in me would not seem so miraculous and merciful.

Without you, I wouldn't feel compassion for hurting and broken people.

Without you, I wouldn't be desperate—desperate for understanding and healing, desperate for a God who is desperate for me.

As you write your letter, be patient with yourself. You may not immediately see the gifts that your brokenness invites into your life. Ask God why he allowed the brokenness. As you remain open for him to unveil his love for you—even, and perhaps especially, in your brokenness—you will begin to hear his intimate answer. This can be a slow process, but I suspect that deep down you know that there has to be a better way than living in the shame of hiding.

The Gift of Relational Failure

When our relationships are the mirror we use to tell ourselves who we are, a failing relationship reflects an image that tells us that we are failures too. Women often go to great lengths to keep from acknowledging the breakdown of a relationship. We deny, diminish, or ignore painful realities. We lie or cover up bad behavior. We become paralyzed because we don't want to lose what we have, even if it is broken. Failure to acknowledge the brokenness in our relationships keeps us from the gift that all this relational messiness can bring. I learned about this gift from a friend of mine named Sara.

Sara is a beautiful woman who makes everyone feel welcome and at ease. She listens intently and seldom offers advice, but I always leave her presence feeling more at peace than with any other person I know. Sara's daughter Carrie broke her heart. Carrie is serving a four-year sentence in the penitentiary.

Sara explained to me that Carrie had always been emotionally volatile but seemed to be getting her life under control, until two years ago. Carrie got into a fight with her boyfriend and seriously injured him. The police were called, and Carrie was arrested and eventually convicted and sentenced to prison.

Sara doesn't look like a woman with a daughter in the penitentiary. She wears clothing from J. Crew. She lives in the suburbs and is a leader in Bible Study Fellowship. Sara told me that when her daughter first got into trouble, she didn't tell anyone. She just hoped that the messy situation would go away. When Carrie went to court, Sara went to the proceedings—alone. When Carrie went into prison, Sara said goodbye, went home, and cried—alone. And then Sara started telling people that Carrie had taken a job in the insurance industry in a faraway city. When people occasionally asked about Carrie, Sara made up some detail about how well her daughter was doing in the insurance business. Once a month, Sara made the three-hour drive to visit Carrie in prison. When she drove away from the penitentiary, she cried all the way home, dried her eyes, and told her friends—if they asked—that her daughter really liked her new job.

Once again, you may be wondering what this dramatic story has to do with you. Sometimes the dramatic stories reveal realities that we all experience on a more subtle level. What do you hide in your relational life and determine to take care of yourself because you have concluded that your reality does not match the agenda you set for yourself? Perhaps your marriage is in trouble, and you and your husband have not talked—really talked—in months. Who do you tell? Why don't you ask for help? When your children disrespect you and you lose your temper or you just give up, where do you go to talk about these realities? When you feel left out by your friends, how do you tell them about your hurt and loneliness? When we deny or dismiss our relational brokenness, we have to harden part of our hearts, and that has consequences.

Sara explained that after lying about her daughter for several months, she no longer talked about anything in her life in authentic ways to anyone, not even to God. We are not compartmentalized beings, so when we ignore the brokenness in our human relationships and harden our hearts to those realities, we will eventually ignore and harden our hearts to the divine relationship as well. We miss another way (a more life-giving way) of living with the painful circumstances in our relationships.

For grace to be grace, it must give us things we didn't know we need and take us to places we didn't want to go.

—Kathleen Norris, *Acedia and Me*

Sara eventually crashed. She got so depressed that she couldn't even get out of bed in the morning. She explained, "I think I had enough integrity to get depressed—to say that my outside life did not at all match my inside life." After seeking counseling, Sara surrendered and began to tell a few close friends the truth about Carrie. In telling the truth about her relational brokenness, she was also telling the truth about herself: she was a woman in pain and in need.

The Exchange: Unrealistic Agendas for Humble Messiness

Humility is the ability to tell the truth about ourselves—nothing more, nothing less. Humility allows us to acknowledge that we are human and, of course, have failed in our relationships but that we are not only failures. Sara confessed that she lied about her daughter because she believed two lies about herself: that *she* couldn't have a daughter in prison and that having a daughter in prison meant

> *We have to embrace the leper within, before we can embrace the leper without.*
>
> —Frances of Assissi

that she was a terrible person. Our relational brokenness reveals that none of us are immune from heartache and difficult relationships.

When we cannot embrace living in humble messiness or cannot let go of our agendas for making everything look good or "work," we miss the rest that comes in surrender. What are your agendas for your relationships? Do you need them to always look good to make you look good? What happens when they break apart? I suspect, if you are like me, you may feel at the end of your rope, lost, desperate, anxious—maybe even like a loser! Who wouldn't want to hide all that or scramble like crazy to make it all somehow work again?

When Sara started to tell the truth about her relational brokenness, she slowly began to experience rest and freedom. She was free to ask for help and support, for herself and for Carrie. She began to travel to the prison twice a month, once to see her daughter and once to participate in a Bible study program for the women. She started to see that these women, including her daughter, were just like her. Out of their desperation and losses, they had made foolish choices, just as Sara did when she lied about Carrie. Out of their pain and anxiety, they cut themselves off from others, just as Sara had. I traveled with Sara one day to the Bible study at the penitentiary. I watched her minister with such grace and tenderness and knew that her brokenness had become a gift to herself and others. When I shared this with her, she said, "I was in prison too — the prison of believing that pain in relationships needed to keep me locked in rather than seeing it as a gift to send me out."

Jesus describes the rest that comes when we exchange our agendas for real, breathing, messy human relationships. He says we are *blessed* when we are broken in our relational lives.

You're blessed when you're at the end of your rope. With less of you there is more of God and his rule.

You're blessed when you feel you've lost what is most dear to you. Only then can you be embraced by the One most dear to you.

You're blessed when you're content with just who you are — no more, no less. That's the moment you find yourselves proud owners of everything that can't be bought.

You're blessed when you've worked up a good appetite for God. He's food and drink in the best meal you'll ever eat.

You're blessed when you care. At the moment of being "care-full," you find yourselves cared for.

You're blessed when you get your inside world — your mind and heart — put right. Then you can see God in the outside world.

—Matthew 5:3–8

If you don't feel blessed, what agenda might you have to exchange to be on the path of surrender?

The Gift of Spiritual Failure

Spiritual failure can be experienced as either our inability to reach God or his inability to reach us. Personal failures and relational failures can certainly catapult us to a place where we feel the absence of God. Maybe you've felt like the psalmist who wrote this:

> God, God ... my God!
> Why did you dump me miles from nowhere?
> Doubled up with pain, I call to God all the day long. No answer.
> Nothing. I keep at it all night, tossing and turning.
> And you! Are you indifferent, above it all, leaning back on the cushions of Israel's praise?
> We know you were there for our parents: they cried for your help and you gave it; they trusted and lived a good life.
> And here I am, a nothing—an earthworm, something to step on, to squash.
> Everyone pokes fun at me; they make faces at me, they shake their heads:
> "Let's see how God handles this one; since God likes him so much, let him help him!"
> —Psalm 22:1–8

These words from Psalm 22 amaze and encourage me. First of all, they are part of a psalm—a song. When was the last time you sang a worship song like this? We tend to hide even our spiritual brokenness, believing that when we worship, it needs to sound like we've got it together. I believe that God gave us this psalm and many other songs of lament in the book of Psalms to teach us that when we speak the truth to God about our spiritual hurt and confusion, it's *worship*. Hiding our spiritual brokenness not only robs us of authentic spirituality; it also robs God of our true worship. To confess your spiritual brokenness, try reading the Psalms as a hymnbook.

The second thing I love about Psalm 22 is that these words

foretell the words of Jesus. When he hung on the cross—body broken and blood shed—he experienced a spiritual brokenness that we cannot fathom. The New Testament tells us that "Jesus groaned out of the depths, crying loudly ... 'My God, my God, why have you abandoned me?'" (Matt. 27:45–46). Jesus entered the depths of brokenness so that we might believe that he knows what it is to feel forsaken, even by God. Surely we can surrender to One who invites our lament so that we might share in the fellowship of his suffering (see Phil. 3:10).

> *For it seems to me that the greatest honour which a soul can pay to God is simply to surrender itself to him.*
>
> —Julian of Norwich, *Showings*

The Exchange: My Way for the Way, the Truth, and the Life

When you are experiencing spiritual brokenness, confess it to the One who understands. Sing his songs. As you worship, you will gradually let go of your way and begin to want the One who is the way, the truth, and the life more than you want your relationships to work.

Treating God Like God

As I shared with you at the beginning of this chapter, my life seems to run in a cycle of working myself into exhaustion only to collapse; that is *my* way. When I collapse, I am tempted to hide, to deny the realities of my life because they don't meet the agenda I think I should live up to, and to fear that God has abandoned me. I know that I am in the midst of brokenness, but I resist surrender. Personal, relational, and spiritual failure taunt me that nothing good can come from all this brokenness.

One collapse took me to the office of a counselor named

Tino. Tino is a lot younger than I am, and I immediately wanted to dismiss him as someone who wouldn't be able to help me. After all, I'm special, complicated, and certainly in need of the most brilliant and seasoned of counselors!

I can't really explain what happened during my appointments with Tino. He told me that he was simply going to talk to me as one alcoholic to another, as one lover of Jesus to another, as one broken person to another. He freely acknowledged his inexperience in counseling, his

In the light of Calvary, how can anything I do be called sacrifice?

—Amy Carmichael, *If*

powerlessness over his own addictions, and his need to surrender daily to One greater than himself. He talked about Jesus as if they really knew each other and related to each other in the mundane, daily realities of life. He quoted familiar Scriptures that I had memorized, probably before he was out of middle school! I rolled my eyes at him, dismissed some of his questions, and explained to him that I *taught* the material he had asked me to read. Tino responded never out of power or control but always out of powerlessness and humility. He modeled the exchanged life: his way exchanged for the Way.

Slowly, another Way—Jesus—manifested to me through Tino. I knew that it was Jesus because I began to leave our counseling sessions thinking not about myself or my counselor but about Jesus. I became willing to be led where I really didn't want to go (that's surrender). I was able to confess—without shame—my self-hatred, arrogance, hard heart, and disobedience. Time and again I was surprised by truths that were not new. Two revelations completely undid me and moved my heart closer to surrender, allowing me to confess my spiritual failures and exchange my way for God's.

During one of our times together, Tino told me about

trying to manage life on his own, being convicted about it, and *apologizing* to God. Something about his humble confession and treatment of God reminded me of a passage in the New Testament: "People knew God perfectly well, but when they didn't treat him like God, refusing to worship him, they trivialized themselves into silliness and confusion so that there was neither sense nor direction left in their lives" (Rom. 1:21). I left that counseling session knowing that I had a lot of things I needed to apologize for.

I need to surrender daily to treating God like God. Treating God like God means inviting him into every part of my life. It includes confessing my darkness to his light. I often begin my day by sitting in my office and telling him the truth: "I don't feel I have anything to offer" or "I really don't have a lot of faith in you today." I often hear God's Spirit in my spirit, kindly answering, "I know." We cannot underestimate how freeing it is to simply tell God the truth.

Treating God like God simply means acknowledging him in the daily realities of our lives. A few years ago, I spoke at a youth event in the Midwest and talked with several hundred young people about addiction. After the final session, one young man shared his story with me and explained the truth that kept him in recovery. He said, with tears streaming down his face, "I decided that maybe Jesus really meant it when he said in the New Testament, 'Every time you eat or drink, do it in remembrance of me.' So that's what I do. I remember him every time I eat or drink." Wow! That sounds simple, but if we really lived like that, the results in our lives would be profound.

Treating God like God means surrendering to being with him in the difficult, daily, and disappointing realities of our lives, not so that he will make everything better but so that we can just be in relationship with him. I'm afraid that too many days I get up and live as if I can do my life without God. That is a dark place, and today I am grateful for spiritual failure because it reveals that I cannot save myself. I need a Savior. God, in his mercy, allows difficult circumstances and realities to reveal our vulnerability to trying to make life work our way. When our way of doing things falls apart, we are in the perfect place to be converted to want the Way, and wanting him more than wanting our own way is a truly surrendered life.

The second revelation in my work with Tino is so sacred that I hesitate to write about it. I do so only because I want to remind myself often — I need to remind myself often — of the life-changing power found in a real relationship with Jesus. Tino told me that if he could give me his own surrender to replace the chaos of hiding, unrealistic agendas, and doing things my way, he would do it. I remember thinking, *Who does this? Who gives up his own peace for another?* And then, of course, I thought of Jesus, who gave up his own life in exchange for mine. "He took the punishment, and that made us whole. Through his bruises we get healed.... And God has piled all our sins, everything we've done wrong, on him, on him" (Isaiah 53:5–6). I couldn't talk after Tino told me of this gift he wanted to give me. I left our session, cried, prayed, and apologized for resisting surrender to the One who exchanged his very life for mine. Surely I can surrender when I know, heart and soul, that Jesus surrendered for me. He became broken so that he might find me in my brokenness.

The gift of brokenness is that it can compel us to surrender. What a relief to know that all this brokenness means something when we become willing to exchange hiding for being known, our agendas for humble messiness, and our way for God's way. There is real rest in discovering that I am completely known and unreservedly loved, that real relationships with others and God only grow in messiness, never according to agendas, and that trusting God's way is the way to discover the love we've been looking for all our lives.

Reflect for a few minutes on what might be missing in your life. Do you feel that no one really knows you? Are you exhausted from always trying to do things right and keep it all together? Are you tired of being resentful because life is not working? Answering yes to any of these questions could reveal a need to surrender. Surrender can seem risky, but it actually is the safest place to be.

The Safety of Brokenness

God uses our brokenness to lure us out of hiding, to teach us to live humbly in the midst of messiness, and to lead us to abandon our ways of making life work for a relationship with the One who is the way, the truth, and the life. When it seems as if nothing is working in your relational life, could you consider the brokenness as a safety net? It is a net that cannot fail! It shows up during seasons of great guilt and pain due to personal failure, relational failure, and spiritual failure. As we fall into this safety net and surrender, we discover that *the* life is found not at the top, where everything looks good, but rather down at the bottom, in the ruins of our brokenness. Climbing the ladder to success—trying to deny, hide, or dismiss our brokenness—almost guarantees that we will miss Christ, who "set aside the privileges of deity and took on the status of a slave" (Phil. 2:7). And when we miss him, we miss everything.

Just for You

---

1. How have unrealistic expectations created a sense of brokenness in your life?

2. Describe the broken part of you that you keep hidden or locked in the basement of your life.

3. Have you ever come out of hiding? Reflect on that experience and how it might have impacted, negatively or positively, your transparency today.

4. What have the failures in your relationships tempted you to believe about yourself?

5. Write your own beatitude based on Matthew 5. For example, "I'm blessed because I'm at the end of my rope with my daughter. With less of me knowing what to do, God has more room to take over. It is up to him."

6. Can you apologize to God for any of your internal realities (pride, a hard heart, dishonesty about your relationships)? If you can't apologize, why not?

7. Read and meditate on Isaiah 53. How does the brokenness of Christ minister to you in your brokenness?

CHAPTER THREE

The Hope of Strange Women

The women, deep in wonder and full of joy, lost no
time in leaving the tomb. They ran to tell the disciples. Then Jesus met them, stopping them in their
tracks. "Good morning!" he said. They fell to their
knees, embraced his feet, and worshiped him.

—Matthew 28:8–9

THERE WAS BLOOD EVERYWHERE. I really had no idea that
it would be like this, so painful and so messy. Pain and mess
are two things I try to avoid at all costs, and there I was in
excruciating agony and a humiliating mess. It was August 29,
1986. I was in Lutheran Hospital about to give birth to my
firstborn, Kristin Marie Hersh. I was in labor for over twenty-
four hours. Family and medical personnel tried to soothe me
and stared at me as I cried, screamed, grunted, and explained
that this would be the only baby I would ever have! Doctors
probed and pushed, and we all willed for this baby to just
come out. Finally, in the early morning hours of August 30,

Kristin arrived. She was coated with blood and mucus. Her head was covered with dark hair that was matted to her scalp. Part of the umbilical cord was dangling from her stomach. Her eyes were glued shut with amniotic fluid.

She was the most beautiful thing I had ever seen.

When the doctors finally placed her on my chest, my heart was beating so fiercely I was afraid it just might bounce her off of me. I didn't know that it was possible to love someone so much, someone who at that moment was absolutely good for nothing. She was just good.

—◌⟩

My friend Elaine has never married. She is fifty years old and has known more suffering than anyone I know. Hers is a story of such horrific abuse that to try to write the details would only minimize the horrors she has witnessed and experienced. Elaine works two jobs, rents out part of her home to supplement her income, and still barely has enough to make ends meet. Twice a year, she travels to Africa to help build orphanages for babies whose lives have been ravaged by AIDS. But while she's there, she also sits for hours not producing anything of economic consequence. She simply sits and rocks motherless babies, quietly singing to them of realities money cannot buy. Perhaps the strangest thing about Elaine is that she owns a wedding dress. She's never been engaged and she doesn't have a boyfriend, but her beautiful white wedding dress hangs on the back of her bedroom door. She spent money that she didn't have for something that she didn't need. The wedding dress is Elaine's symbol of hope.

—◌⟩

I met Raeann at a weekly Twelve Step meeting that I attend. Raeann grew up in Oklahoma and moved to Denver when she was nineteen years old. When Raeann couldn't find work, she slowly drifted to a part of town and a way of life that often welcomes the destitute and desperate. She started using drugs and alcohol to numb her disappointment and fear, and then she started letting others use her so that she could make enough money to keep her in the prison that her life had become. Raeann has now been out of the sex-trade nightmare and in recovery for over five years. She rents a room from an elderly woman who lives in that downtrodden part of town. Raeann works for a dry cleaner thirty hours a week and makes about seven dollars an hour. Every week at our meeting, I listen to well-meaning fellow attendees give Raeann tips about better jobs. They are waiting for her recovery to "kick in" so that she can begin to do something that looks more successful. I smile as I watch Raeann humbly navigate their coaching. I know that she's not looking for success. Her simple life allows her to spend three hours every day in a chapel next to a large downtown church. I've asked her what she does during those three hours. She always answers the same: "I sing a little and pray a lot. We have a lot to talk about." Raeann also spends four nights a week on the same streets that once sold her to strangers. She now hands out peanut butter sandwiches, warm gloves in the winter, and bottles of water in the summer to other women caught in a life that they would have never chosen.

—☙

These are three stories about strange women. The dictionary defines *strange* as "surprising and alien." Because we are designed for relationships but live in a world that shatters our dreams, breaks our hearts, and compels us to surrender control, we are going to feel alien at times in a culture that advises us to play it safe and look out for ourselves. And we will be desperate for a surprise of grace, mercy, and joy along the way. As we look further at these three women, perhaps you will be able to identify with their surprising and at times alien stories. Maybe you will even discover that you are strange too!

The Hope in Looking Like a Fool

All three of these strange women seem a little foolish. Their stories include failure and disappointment, but they are not hiding in shame. They find joy in small, messy realities. They are not energized by climbing the ladder to success but seem content in places where they might not be noticed. Even though none of these women will probably ever grace the cover of *People* magazine, something about each story makes us pause and ask, "What really gives life meaning?" The stories of these strange women show the compelling hope found in looking like a fool—the hope of being loved when we are good for nothing, the hope of security in a relationship that cannot fail, and the hope of handing out hope to other strange women.

My Story: Being Loved When We Are Good for Nothing

When I gave birth to Kristin (and eighteen months later to my son, Graham), I was surprised by love and experienced at a deep level the truest meaning of love: wanting someone when they are good for nothing. In a culture built on production and performance, loving someone when they are good for nothing is an alien idea; it flies in the face of everything we have come to believe about worth. But don't you hope that a mother's love for her baby is symbolic of something truer than our fast-paced, dog-eat-dog, competitive world? I don't know about you, but I long to be loved not for what I do but for who I am, even when I am good for nothing. My love for my children is a faithful reminder that I am strange; I will endure pain for relationship, find hope in a mess, look like a fool again and again, and learn about love from a baby who can't do anything but cry, eat, and need her diapers changed!

When was the last time that you knew, really knew, that you are loved for who you are, not for what you do? As women, we often get caught in the "golden handcuffs" of being caregivers. When our identity becomes dependent on caring for others, we place ourselves in a destructive bind. When those we care for are doing well, we are tempted to believe it is because we are so good to them, and then we feel pressure to keep on being really good. When those we care for aren't doing well, we may believe that it's because we are bad, and once again we feel pressure, thinking that if only we could be better, then they would be better. Trusting in God's goodness unlocks the handcuffs. He loves us because he is good. He loves us and those we care for even when we are good for nothing, because he is love. It is his nature to love us. He loves us whether we are in a state of grace or disgrace. When we believe that we are loved even when we are good for nothing, we can rest from all our striving. That's freedom.

Elaine's Story: The Security of a Relationship That Cannot Fail

Elaine's story is surprising because the terrible abuse she experienced did not stop her. It does not define her. In fact, it takes her to the places where the last and the least live, and it has opened her heart to love the most unloved. But Elaine's story is strange. Why would she buy that wedding dress when she often doesn't have enough money to pay all of her bills? Elaine's ideas about security are foolish. She's not trying to accumulate enough success or accolades to feel safe, and that's strange, because if anyone should long for safety and security, it's Elaine. But she longs for something else. She longs to be so in love that even if her life looks a little ridiculous, she doesn't care.

In the New Testament, Jesus said, "I was hungry and you fed me, I was thirsty and you gave me a drink, I was homeless and you gave me a room, I was shivering and you gave me clothes, I was sick and you stopped to visit, I was in prison and you came to me.... Whenever you did one of these things to someone overlooked or ignored, that was me—you did it to me" (Matt. 25:35–36, 40). Elaine really believes these words. She has told me that Jesus fills her life with moments of meaning as she ministers grace to hungry, thirsty, strange, naked, sick, imprisoned people. She really believes she is loving Jesus when she loves others, and she believes he is her Groom. The New Testament does refer to believers as the bride of Christ, but Elaine doesn't rely on theological experts to confirm what she has experienced. God has used her story to romance her to his love and longing to fill her aching heart with love, forgiveness, and healing. She is living for her Groom, who loves her with abandon.

God writes himself into all of our stories, including our stories of love sought, lost, consummated, and abandoned. Every love story is about him. Everyone who looks for love in all the wrong places is telling a story about him. All of our relationships are about him; they foreshadow Christ, who cannot fail. When we believe that human relationships are an end in themselves, we write a smaller story for ourselves. Now might be a good time to reflect on how your human relationships create a need for God. Does considering him your Groom seem too real and too personal? Sometimes we get nervous and turn Jesus into a doctrine, or we want him to be a protector or deliverer but not a lover. Thank goodness for our painful human relationships! They reveal that we need a lover who will remain faithful when we are faithless and who will never leave us or forsake us. When we believe that human relationships are to lead us into a relationship with the One who is the beginning and ending of every story, we discover a larger story, one that is eternal.

Raeann's Story: Handing Out Hope to Other Strange Women

Bride of Christ, stop hiding from Jesus. . . . He came to earth for his bride, a bride who would respond to his advances with the most glorious, free, and uninhibited of passions — his own love.

—Peter Hiett,
Dance Lessons for Zombies

Very few people know Raeann, and only a handful know what fills her hours and days. Raeann is surprising. She is a beautiful woman who is full of insight and compassion. Some with her past story of failure and misery might want to compensate by creating a new life that is full of obvious success, but Raeann doesn't have anything to prove. Success is not even on her radar screen. She explains, "Some people might think my life was a waste and still is. I don't mind wasting it now, though." Strange. This woman who once sold herself for drugs, alcohol, and a fifteen-dollar-a-night motel room now spends herself in worship and care for others. As she moves among the nightlife on East Colfax in Denver, she is an alien presence handing out hope to women like her, strange women who just want to be loved.

How do you offer yourself to the world? When relationships don't work, it is easy to believe that we have nothing to offer. Raeann reminds me that when we are emptied of ourselves, God's presence is most visible. We become God's presence in the world when we invite others to the love of God, a love that is for starving, bleeding, broken people. The good news is that offering hope to others does not begin with what we do for God. It begins with what God does for us. When we know, heart and soul, that he pours out his love on us regardless of how we perform, we have hope to offer to others. It will be natural to sit shoulder to shoulder with other hurting women and give time, attention, compassion, curiosity, prayer, and other acts of service because we know we have been loved.

The Hope of Persisting in Relationships

All women are strange in their persistence in relationships; we are willing to go through great pain and messiness for relationships. Teresa of Avila described her hunger for relationship to be such that she could "eat anyone who offered a taste of friendship." I have read that Teresa's passion scared many of her contemporaries. Carol Gilligan, a feminist researcher and writer, discovered that if female corporate executives are asked to choose between career and relationship, they will almost always choose relationship, even if it means losing their career.[1] For many women, choosing to forgo climbing up the corporate ladder to climb down into the difficulties of relationships doesn't seem like a strange decision. Mary Pipher, therapist and author, concludes that most women will do anything, including becoming mental patients, to preserve relationships.[2]

We don't need ancient manuscripts or research statistics to confirm our longing for relationships and the strange, surprising, and even alien places that our longing takes us. The mother who becomes an expert in espionage to try to understand her children and keep them from harm doesn't care if her children think she's strange; her love eclipses her need to look respectable. The mother who watches her youngest child board the bus for first grade or her oldest pack his bags for college is surprised again by a love that threatens to make her a stalker of her children and leave her heartbroken.

Mothers are not the only ones made strange by love. The woman who learns that she will never conceive and have a baby of her own is terrified that if people could see the longing screaming inside her soul, they would surely shrink back because of its alien intensity. Women who attend relationship seminars and wrap themselves in plastic wrap to keep their marriages alive aren't afraid of being strange if it means a better relationship. Even when a marriage is dying, women are often surprised to find that they can't quit; they hang in there. Nine out of ten women married to men with addictions will stay in their marriage. Conversely, just one out of ten men married to an addicted woman stays with his addicted mate. Women are just strange.

I have a beautiful single friend who works for a global mission organization. She is bright, articulate, and full of zest for life. She posted her picture and biography on a well-known, reputable dating website about a year ago. She has had dating experiences that would fill an entire book. She's gone on dates with a man who didn't speak English, a man who turned out to be fifteen years younger than she is, and a man who asked her to marry him and move to Argentina on the first date! Her "doozies" in the world of dating have not kept her from meeting every week with four other single women to pray about their longing to be married, and she continues to update her profile on the website and to hope that the next date not only will be normal but may be the love of her life.

Whether married or single, a parent or childless, whether or not we acknowledge our longing for relationships, all women experience the strange, surprising, and sometimes alien sensation of wanting more. It haunts us, leads us to buy another book on relationships, or compels us to check the dating website one more time. You know the nagging moments I am talking about, the moments that catch us unaware: loading the dishwasher, waiting to make a left-hand turn, reaching for the mail, or reflecting just before sleep steals the day. A vague uneasiness flits before our eyes, and our hearts again hope that we will experience what we long for: to love and be loved.

Persisting in Hope When Relationships Falter

Our longing to love and be loved and our persistence in relationships that are disappointing or difficult can make it a challenge to keep hope afloat. What does hope look like in the ebb and flow of real relationships? A further look at the three stories we have followed in this chapter reveals that hope takes risks, gives to others, and rests and that the natural ebb and flow of relationships can quickly diminish and distort hope.

Hope takes risks. Hope took me to Lutheran Hospital and, in the midst of pain and mess, compelled me to believe that the thing longed for—a baby—was worth it. In mothering, hope often changes, though. We can move from loving someone when they are good for nothing to needing them to be good for something. Misplaced hope can create agendas and rigid expectations that can come between mother and child. Hope compels us to keep our hands open, to hold loosely, and to look for life in places of change.

Hope gives to others. Hope released Elaine from being stuck as a victim and led her to love others and believe in something for herself. Hope will not allow us to stay in ourselves; it calls us to others. Hope can also make us a little heartsick when we fail, when others fail us, and when relationships just don't work. Desperate hope can lead women to destructive and demeaning relationships and can keep women in abusive relationships that they believe they are destined to stay in forever. Genuine hope allows us to let go of destructive relationships and trust God to meet us in new ways in our loneliness so that we can give to others.

Hope allows us to rest. Hope allows Raeann to worship and work among the ruins of her former life with a contentment that I have rarely observed. In a world that is often careless with our hopes and hearts, living with that kind of hope is a task of heroic proportions. Destroyed hope can drain life from women and keep them from moving forward. We can only keep hope afloat when we rest in a hope that is greater than ourselves.

The ebb and flow of human relationships guarantees that hope will ebb and flow as well. Taking risks, giving to others, and resting will energize hope, but be assured that the moment you take a risk, give to others, or rest, the enemy of your soul will be crouching right around the corner, waiting to steal your hope. Hope is what pulls us forward, and if Satan can steal our hope, we will be stuck. What pulls us out of the mire of misplaced, distorted, or destroyed hope?

Hope Persists When We Cling to Jesus

Whenever I feel shame about being a little strange, I remember the women that Jesus hung out with in the New Testament stories. There was Mary, the virgin mother; single Mary of Magdalene, who was always falling on his feet; the thirsty Samaritan woman who couldn't keep a husband; the sick and grasping rag woman; frantic and grieving Mary, sister of Lazarus; the sentenced adulteress; and the weeping and clinging prostitute. In fact, the only woman in the New Testament who doesn't seem strange is Martha, the other sister of Lazarus. Martha is busy. She is doing something to try to make life work. Jesus gently stops Martha, "Martha, dear Martha, you're fussing far too much and getting yourself worked up over nothing. One thing only is essential, and Mary has chosen it" (Luke 10:41–42). Jesus seems to be encouraging Martha to be like her sister, the strange woman falling on his feet.

When relationships are difficult and are not working, our natural impulse is to work harder or give up. We believe that we have to do something or deaden our hearts to our longings. Our God-given longing for relationships often causes us to fuss and get worked up, relying on ourselves or others to be our source of hope. We need another source, a source that does not drain or diminish us in the difficult realities of relationships. When we look to ourselves or others as the source of hope, we will come up short.

I was reminded of the folly of misplaced hope when my daughter was a senior in high school. She drove a Jeep Wrangler that always seemed to be in the repair shop for one thing or another. Near the end of her senior year, it was yet again at Midas for some work on the brakes. The repairman called to let me know that the cost would be over nine hundred dollars. I hung up the phone and began to cry. My daughter was standing near me, and I explained, "Your Jeep is going to cost almost a thousand dollars to fix. We don't have that money. You're getting ready to go to college, and we have all these costs that we have to save for ..." I became more and more distraught as I explained our economic realities. Kristin's eyes got wider with fear, until she finally interrupted

> *Whom have I in heaven but you? And earth has nothing I desire besides you. My flesh and my heart may fail, but God is the strength [the hope] of my heart and my portion forever.*
>
> —Psalm 73:25–26 NIV

me, "Mom, you need to call the Midas man and tell him to lower his price. My whole future depends on it!" I was caught hoping in myself and the Midas man. I thought that I needed to panic and to come up with a plan to keep hope afloat. I didn't know that hope actually rises when we let go.

The Hope of Letting Go

Intuitively, we often believe that hope requires us to latch on to something, to make something happen, to keep trying so that circumstances will eventually work out, but this often turns hope into something that is desperate, distorted, or destroyed. Hope that pulls us forward in redemptive ways is about letting go. Let's consider the stories of the three strange women we've looked at throughout this chapter and the lessons they teach about letting go of earning love, letting go of security, and letting go of success. Only a strange woman can let go of these things that often feel like life itself, but that's how we know we're on to something. When letting go feels counterintuitive and countercultural, it may also be supernatural.

> But whoever loses his life for me will save it.
>
> —Luke 9:24 NIV

My Story: Letting Go of Earning Love

On a recent flight to Orlando, I sat next to a woman who was traveling to Florida to run a marathon. It took me only a few minutes to identify that she was a serious runner. She had the well-toned legs of a runner, and she carried her most prized possession with her on the airplane: her running shoes. I asked her what she expected her marathon time to be, and when she told me close to four hours, I knew that I would not be sharing with her my nearly seven-hour times in the two marathons I had limped through. I asked her what prompted her to train and to run marathons. I learned that although her times were very different from mine, our motivations for running were similar. "It is something in my life that I can conquer," she explained, "and that feels good!"

I understood. I ran my first marathon shortly after my marriage fell apart. With every step of the 26.2 miles, I told myself, "I can do hard things." There is nothing wrong with attaining goals, mastering difficult circumstances, and over-coming overwhelming obstacles, but these are not the source of hope. They trick us into believing that we are the creators and maintainers of hope. They taunt us that we need to hang on to our achievements, our gifts, our money, our accomplish-ments—ourselves—for dear life. It seems to be the American spirit to manage calamities and crises by focusing on what we can do. We even elected a president who gave us the mantra "Yes we can!" I think I joined in the hopeful national chorus of "Yes we can!" because so often I have experienced the oppo-site personal reality: "No I can't."

I have felt powerless in my relationships, in my behav-iors, and in all my efforts to prove that I am good enough to be worthy of love and to protect myself from being hurt. I remember crying out to a dear friend, "Why do I have to be so powerless—a lonely, fearful, insecure, and needy woman? Why can't I make these realities go away?" He responded qui-etly and simply to my angst, "Have you ever asked God that?" Quite honestly, my first internal response to his question was a mocking answer, "No, I've never asked God that." I think my cynicism was partly a fear that God wouldn't answer and partly a fear of how he has already answered.

The New Testament reveals without apology God's love for those who are powerless: "Many who are first will be last, and many who are last will be first" (Matt. 19:30 NIV); "If you want to find your life, you need to lose it" (Mark 8:35, my paraphrase). The New Testament words of Jesus all point to the hope in powerlessness. No wonder I didn't want to ask God about the presence of powerlessness in my life. At some level, I already knew that it was a gift from him to teach me about the hope of letting go, especially of letting go of my need to earn love. When we respond to powerlessness by trying to prove that we are good enough, strong enough, and worthy enough of love, we will lose hope. Ironically, our effort to flee powerlessness is the very thing that leads to a loss of all hope.

We resist powerlessness because it frustrates our determination to do something and to feel in control. Ask the couple who has been married for twenty years, has four kids, and cannot figure out how to love each other again. Their histories, the wounds they've inflicted on each other, and the temptation to believe that the grass really is greener elsewhere all fuel their powerlessness to remain committed to their vows. In other words, their determination to do something actually makes their problem worse. It weakens their relationship and makes them vulnerable to infidelity.

Powerlessness is a gift that makes our hands bleed when we open it, so we often hide this gift in a dark, locked room in the basement of our lives. Could powerlessness really be the gift to reveal where we are intended to find hope? On some days, I believe that it could be. On those days, I can see a few gifts that a powerlessness-driven life is revealing to me, gifts that are all about hope.

Powerlessness Can Propel Me to Let Go

Richard Rohr writes, "The only ones who can accept the path of Jesus are those who have nothing to protect, not their own self-image or their reputation, their possessions, their theology, their principles, or their certitude."[3] As we say in

Alcoholics Anonymous, when we let go, we can let God; we can let God love us for who we are, not what we do. Rohr continues, "The Gospels say very clearly that God loves imperfect, powerless people. But it's only the imperfect and broken who can believe that. Thus it happens that God throws a party—and the "good" people don't come. That's why God says that cripples, the lame, and the blind are to be invited—and they would be ready."[4] Powerlessness allows us to give up being dependent on a perfectible self and to become dependent on a God who not only loves imperfect people but invites them to intimacy. Hope is born in believing that God loves me when I'm good for nothing.

> *He presented himself for this sacrificial death when we were far too weak and rebellious to do anything to get ourselves ready. . . . But God put his love on the line for us by offering his Son in sacrificial death while we were of no use whatever to him."*
>
> —Romans 5:6, 8

Powerlessness Can Compel Me to Love Others for More Than What They Can Do for Me

We are more likely to let other people in and to move outside of ourselves when we are broken and unashamed of our brokenness. The mystery and vulnerability of powerlessness is that we connect with other powerless people. I don't know about you, but I am drawn to people who have suffered, people who are twisted out of shape, and people who limp through marathons, but I have to embrace my own suffering, my misshapen life, and my limping before I can embrace it in others. I am discovering that I am powerless to produce this act of compassion, but powerlessness makes room for the gift of compassion and for real relationships that are not based on performance. Hope grows as I stop requiring others to be something for me.

Powerlessness Invites Us to an Intimate Relationship with a Power Greater Than Ourselves

When I finally followed my friend's gentle suggestion and asked God, "Why do I have to experience powerlessness?" I began to hear an answer: I have to experience powerlessness so that I might be loved, love others, and experience radical hope that is dependent not on my hanging on but on my letting go.

One more part to this evolving answer came while I was reading the story of the powerless, prodigal son in Luke 15. His self-reliant older brother had not yet experienced powerlessness. He thought he had done a pretty good job of proving himself to the father and was frustrated that the father gave a party for the wayward, good-for-nothing brother. Robert Capon, an Episcopal priest, writes about this New Testament story. He explains that the older brother was invited to the party too. The father went out to the field to invite the competent brother. When the brother refused, determined to stay in the hell of his own effort, Capon imagines the father saying, "Stop it! Just stop it. This isn't about bookkeeping. It's about life and death."[5]

I can imagine the Father tenderly and sternly answering my question, "Why do I have to be powerless?" by saying, "Sharon, just stop it. Stop proving yourself. Stop protecting yourself. This isn't about saving yourself or earning love. It's about dying and it's about resurrection." Powerlessness becomes the path to life. The source of hope for my desire to love and be loved lies in compelling me to let go (to die) and let God (to be resurrected). If I believe that God loves me when I'm good for nothing, then I can love him because he is good. This circle of give-and-take becomes the source of hope.

Elaine's Story: Letting Go of Security

Every time Elaine looks at her wedding dress, she remembers that her security is found not in an earthly relationship but in an eternal reality. She is the bride of Christ. The strange purchase of her wedding dress reminds her that eternal realities are more real than earthly realities. We constantly get confused about this. We believe that being pursued by Christ, being loved by Christ, and being joined to him for eternity is the consolation prize. We believe that relationships on earth are the prize, so we place all our hope in them. Letting go of security doesn't mean that we drop out of life, hide in our bedrooms, and watch hours of reality TV. Letting go means that we believe, heart and soul, that nurturing a relationship with Jesus is the prize.

> *Christ's love makes [us] whole. . . . Everything he does and says is designed to bring the best out of her, dressing her in dazzling white silk, radiant with holiness.*
>
> —Ephesians 5:26–27

Several months ago, Elaine learned that she had thyroid cancer. My heart sank as I heard her news, and I wondered how she could bear one more blow in her life. I have watched Elaine navigate her latest trial with grace and confusion, peace and anxiety, faith and doubt. Elaine has poured herself into human relationships, ministry, and self-care, but that certainly has not resulted in security for her. The truth is that human relationships, ministry, and self-care will inevitably fail us and bog us down in the quagmire of a life that isn't working. And that's where hope gets stuck.

Part of Elaine's treatment required that she spend days in isolation due to her radiation therapy. I asked Elaine about her time alone. She explained that she had read 1 Corinthians 13 (the "Love Chapter" in the New Testament) over and over again. She looked at each descriptor of love and journaled about nurturing those attributes in her relationship with Jesus. Elaine explained to me that she got the idea for looking at the Love Chapter from a film that is popular right now among married couples. The movie, *Fireproof*, encourages couples to use 1 Corinthians 13 and its description of love to challenge and change their marriages. I was immediately challenged by Elaine's relentless return to her relationship with Jesus. I was amazed that rather than turning from this "couples' exercise" with bitterness and resentment, she turned to Jesus. I so often live as if he's the consolation prize, thinking that being in a relationship with him won't make much of a difference in my life and that he'll always be there waiting, so why not concentrate on getting a more tangible prize? Elaine's experience continues to compel me to want Jesus most.

As an example, Elaine explained that for "Love doesn't want what it doesn't have" (1 Cor. 13:4), she meditated on that description of love and thought about all her complaints against God for not giving her what she wanted. She asked God for a heart that would hope in him, not in the gifts that he gives. She made a list of everything she was grateful for. She explained that she had a lot of time to talk to God, and as she did, her hope shifted from getting what she wanted to wanting to love him. I could imagine myself sitting in isolation making lists of all that I needed to do when I got out. Elaine invested in a love relationship, not in shopping lists or to-do lists.

As I once again watched my friend let go of security during her health crisis, I saw that being in love with Jesus is Elaine's security. She persists in hope because she nurtures a relationship with him every day. Strange women remain hopeful in calamities and crises because they know that they are in a relationship that holds them.

Elaine has navigated a tragic past and continues to walk through some tricky trials, but she is committed to creating a life of compassion, which comes out of her intimate relationship with Jesus. She offers hope to other victims of painful circumstances because she knows that hope isn't found in circumstances. Hope is a relationship. She has a wedding dress on the back of her bedroom door to prove it.

Raeann's Story: Letting Go of Success

Raeann is the only woman I know whose life resembles that of the strange woman who poured perfume on Jesus' feet. Raeann finds hope in worshiping Jesus during her times of prayer and singing and in providing clothing and food to the prostitutes on East Colfax. Raeann beams with hope, and after reading the New Testament story of the woman who poured perfume on Jesus' feet, I think I know why Raeann beams. The disciples were indignant that this strange woman was spending herself and her resources in ways that seemed good for nothing, but Jesus told them, "She has just done something wonderfully significant for me" (Matt. 26:10). Hope comes when we find our significance only in what we do for Jesus. God made us for relationships, but when we find our significance in how well they work or in how good our lives look, we are at risk of losing hope. Human relationships are not reliable sources of hope. When I spend myself for Jesus in my relationships and other activities, I am filled with hope.

How do we know whether we are doing something for Jesus or trying to prove ourselves by our good deeds? Raeann has taught me that there are two hallmarks of a woman who is serving Jesus rather than serving herself. The first is that she has experienced redemption in her story. I never sense any shame from Raeann when she talks about her past. She knows that she is forgiven. That's important, because when she ministers to women who are still in the clutches of bondage, she never judges. Her compassion and care are beacons of hope to women lost in shame. Raeann illustrates the truth in the New Testament story about the woman who poured perfume on Jesus' feet. Jesus told his disciples, "Her many sins have been forgiven—for she loved much" (Luke 7:47 NIV).

The second hallmark of a woman who is living for Jesus is that she is offering to others for their sakes, not hers. Whenever we spend our energy to fill up our emptiness, we get caught up in needing something to happen for us. One night I went with Raeann to give food and water on the streets. When she suggested that I stand back and watch for a while, I was a bit offended. She didn't think I was capable of handing out water bottles? After about an hour of watching, I approached Raeann. I commented on my observations so far, "I guess the women are grateful, but I haven't heard anyone say 'Thank you.'" I cringe at what my comments revealed about myself. Raeann gently answered, "I'm not doing

Do you see this woman? I came to your home; you provided no water for my feet, but she rained tears on my feet and dried them with her hair. You gave me no greeting, but from the time I arrived she hasn't quit kissing my feet. You provided nothing for freshening up, but she has soothed my feet with perfume. Impressive isn't it?

—Luke 7:44–47

this because I need something in return. I'm here because they really need food and water."

Raeann's significance is found in her experience of redemption, and her offering to others is out of gratitude for her own salvation. No wonder she is such a hopeful woman. Her significance is not rooted in herself but is dependent on the give-and-take of love. She has been loved, so she loves others.

The Hope of Strange Women

Perhaps you have felt frustrated while reading this chapter. When you find yourself wondering what you can do to make your relationships work, can you consider surrendering to a different goal? When making our lives work is our goal, we will fight a constant battle with hope. We will need to be good enough, to have enough, and to do enough. We will be full of our own dreams and schemes and be perpetually exhausted and frustrated. Letting go takes courage. It means daring to believe that being loved by Jesus, finding our security in him, and discovering our significance in worshiping him are enough.

When I surrender to loving Jesus and being loved by him as the goal of my life, then when I'm in relational difficulties, I have great hope. When others misjudge me, I have great hope. When I am lonely, I have great hope. When I am powerless, I know I am in the perfect place for hope to grow. When I am disappointed, I have great hope. Do you see? Every relational difficulty, disappointment, or disaster is an opportunity to love him more, trust him more, and worship him more. When our goal changes from making relationships work to wanting a more intimate relationship with Jesus, we not only have hope, but we are ready to face difficulties in relationships with greater clarity.

Romans 4 says it this way: "But if you see that the job is too big for you, that it's something only *God* can do, and you trust him to do it—you could never do it for yourself no matter how hard and long you worked—well, that trusting-him-to-do-it is what gets you set right with God, *by* God. Sheer gift" (Rom. 4:5, italics added). Powerlessness, insecurity, and relational upheaval are gifts from God to compel us to let go. This week, when you encounter pain, mess, and heartache, try whispering this prayer: "Oh, I hope this makes me trust you more, love you more, and worship you more." As strange as it may seem, you will be becoming a woman of hope.

I sat with a group of five women friends in my kitchen one summer, talking as only women can about our marriages, our recipes, and our relationships. We acknowledged our longings, admitted our foolishness, and decided that all that we want in relationships can make us a little strange. We laughed at the possibilities of living with a longing for love and ending up in the psych ward, wearing our bathrobes all day and doing crossword puzzles. Then someone remembered the words of Teresa of Avila—yes, the same strange woman who wrote of her devouring longing for relationships. She also wrote, "May I be mad with love for him, who for love of me became mad."[6] The kitchen table became an altar where we bowed our strange hearts for a few moments and worshiped an even stranger God.

Just for You

1. Describe some surprising and even alien experiences you've had in relationships.What do these experiences reveal about you—about your courage, faith, creativity, and resilience?

2. Think of a relationship when you loved someone even if they were good for nothing. What does that experience reveal about how God feels about you?

3. Write a story or draw a picture that illustrates how you feel when you are powerless.

4. What makes you feel most secure? What or who would you trust if you lost that security?

5. What makes you feel significant? How would your life change if you suddenly lost that source of significance?

6. Write about a time of brokenness in your life. How would you have wanted someone to minister to you during this time? How can you now minister to others because of what you have experienced?

7. Read the descriptors of love in 1 Corinthians 13. How can you nurture these attributes in your relationship with Jesus?

PART 2

Begin Again, Believe Again
in Difficult Relationships

I was frantic to help Nic, to stop his descent, to save my son. This, mixed with my guilt and worry, consumed me.... When my child was born, it was impossible to imagine he would suffer in the ways Nic has suffered.

—David Sheff,
Beautiful Boy

The discovery that Christians can be cruel to Christians has destroyed the spiritual life of many a believer's life. I would dare say that truly vicious attacks on the part of one believer to another leaves most Christians so hurt they never fully recover.

—Gene Edwards,
Exquisite Agony

Life is pain, life is only pain. We're all taught to believe in happy, fairy-tale endings, but there is only blackness, dark depressing loneliness that eats away at your soul.

—Carrie,
Sex and the City

We learn pretty quickly that pain in relationships is inevitable. Just ask my ten-year-old client who was the only girl in her fifth-grade class not invited to "the popular girl's" slumber party. Divorce, infertility, chronic illness, loss, and even betrayal by lifelong friends can leave us reeling, determined that we will never want another relationship again.

Chapter 4 encourages the braverheart to feel the pain of humiliation when her dreams shatter, her life falls through the cracks, and she becomes the subject of gossip and suspicion. Strangely, it is in this place of seeming disgrace that she learns the wisdom of tenderness. She discovers that the gift of kindness, arising from the ashes of humiliation, is the gift this fast-paced, dehumanized world is most hungry for.

Sometimes humiliation takes us a step farther than just failure in relationships and leaves us in the heart-shattering place of estrangement from family and friends. In chapter 5 we will look at this painful experience, when everything within us screams, "This is not how it is supposed to be!" The desert of estrangement can become a place where we discover the grace of desperation, which allows us to pray and really mean and actually live the words of Jesus' disciples when they faced estrangement from peers and the religious establishment: "Master, to whom would we go? You have the words of real life, eternal life" (John 6:68). Estrangement becomes the sacred context for experiencing crucifixion and resurrection, truly being transformed into Jesus' image.

For some, difficult relationships become experiences that we believe are unbearable. The loss of a child, the imprisonment of a son, the double life of a husband who announces his sexual indiscretion and betrayal, the marriage that suffers another ten years without romance are all experiences that leave us in the grip of loneliness. In chapter 6, we will consider how loneliness can either trap us in a dungeon or become the place of our greatest fruitfulness. When we no longer see loneliness as a curse or a punishment, we discover the ruins of our relationships are where God's presence abides and the most beautiful fruit grows.

CHAPTER FOUR

The Valley of Humiliation

To be convinced of my acceptance, I must know that
I am accepted at my worst.

—Sebastian Moore,
The Crucified Jesus Is No Stranger

THE WIGGLY FIRST GRADERS lined up in the center of the
stage. It was the spring assembly, and all the parents strained
to spot their six-year-old during the program. We watched
them sing, act out short skits about springtime, and recite
poems they had memorized. I nearly burst with pride as I
watched my daughter, Kristin, standing erect, hands at her
sides, singing passionately without missing a word. At one
point in the program, the teacher explained that the class had
completed a learning unit about careers. Different parents had
spoken to the class about their occupations. I recalled Kristin
coming home and talking about Jennifer's dad, a policeman,
and Nicole's mom, who baked wedding cakes. The teacher

explained that each class member would now step forward and tell what they hoped to be when they grew up.

The parents edged forward in their seats as they waited for their son or daughter to step up to the microphone. Many in this class of first graders wanted to be veterinarians. I wondered if Kristin would also choose to be a veterinarian. She had always longed for a dog but had to settle for goldfish because of my allergies. A few of the squirmy six-year-olds wanted to be teachers. I imagined that their career choice made their teacher proud. In between teaching them to read and overseeing games of dodgeball, she had inspired them to be like her.

Kristin was the second to last to announce her career choice. She walked up to the microphone and surveyed the audience. I was amazed at her poise. I imagined her explaining that she wanted to be a public speaker because she knew that I spoke at a few church events. Maybe she'd express a desire to be a writer. She'd seen me hunched over my journal almost every morning, writing my thoughts and dreams for the future. Kristin spotted me in the middle of the auditorium, and her eyes locked on mine.

"When I grow up ..." She paused, and I held my breath. "... I want to be nothing—just like my mom!"

Everyone was quiet for what seemed like five minutes, and then I heard a few giggles. I slowly crumbled into my chair, wishing I could hide under the seat. I didn't know whether to laugh or cry. I knew that my face was turning red, and I was just sure that everyone was trying to find the mom in the crowd who was *nothing*. I wondered if I could post my résumé on the school bulletin board the next day to prove that my daughter was wrong; I was *something*.

Even as I recall this story years later, humiliation floods through me. Humiliation seeps in when we believe that we said the wrong thing, did the wrong thing, or are the wrong thing. *Shame* is a synonym for *humiliation*. A distinctive aspect of humiliation is that it requires the eyes of another; we feel disgraced or embarrassed because others have seen our failures or limitations. Humiliation haunts us and convinces us to scramble like crazy to prove something, to prove that we are *someone*. Kristin's announcement to an auditorium filled with proud parents and other family members that I was *nothing* got right to the heart of humiliation. The dictionary defines *humiliation* as "loss of face." Loss of face implies losing one's self-image. When my daughter declared that I was nothing, the humiliation I felt came from a core fear that if I didn't have a lot of external accomplishments to prop me up, I would be discovered as a nothing, a nobody. I knew that somewhere in the midst of Kristin's humiliating answer was a compliment (she wanted to be like me!), but any affirmation in our life quickly dissipates and leaves us needing more to cover up our deficiencies.

> *I'm nobody. Who are you?*
> *Are you nobody too?*
>
> —Emily Dickinson,
> "I'm Nobody! Who Are You?"

Relational Humiliation

I suspect you know what *relational humiliation* means. We can be feeling pretty good about our lives, and then, almost like a pin popping a balloon, the difficulties or disappointments in our relationships burst our bubble and taunt us that we don't know what we're doing, we can't make life work, and even when we do, it's just a cover-up for a whole lot of nothingness. Think about how quickly humiliation intrudes in situations like these:

- Your daughter announces that she hates her life and it's *your* fault.

- Your friends plan a girls' night out and don't invite you.
- Your husband forgets your anniversary.
- Someone in your book club greets you by the wrong name.
- You get to work and notice that you have unmatched shoes.
- You click on Facebook and note that you have only thirty-six friends.

These are just a few familiar humiliations, and the shame from them fades pretty quickly. But some humiliations pierce our hearts and get stuck there. As we begin to look at difficult relationships, the valley of humiliation is a good place to start. Perhaps our best guide for this journey is the biblical story of Esther, a woman who faced her relational humiliation with remarkable courage and faith.

Esther is a woman who can inspire us to walk through humiliating circumstances with our heads held high and our hearts open to others and to God. Her story is relevant because it features many of the contexts that still have the potential to humiliate women today: our place in society, in our homes, at work, in God's work, and in relationships with ourselves, others, and God. Although God is never mentioned in Esther's story, God's heart is so evident that we cannot miss it; we must not miss it.

Orphan, Stranger, Outcast

Here is how the Bible begins Esther's story: "This is the story of something that happened in the time of Xerxes ... who ruled from India to Ethiopia.... Now there was a Jew who lived in the palace complex in Susa. His name was Mordecai.... His ancestors had been taken from Jerusalem with the exiles and carried off ... by King Nebuchadnezzar of

Babylon into exile. Mordecai had reared his cousin Hadassah, otherwise known as Esther, since she had no father or mother" (Est. 1:1, 2:5–7).

Note how one of the first things the text describes is Esther's relational status. According to every mark of significance in her patriarchal culture, Esther was a nobody, an exile with virtually no family. In Esther's time, that was a very humiliating state for a woman to find herself in.

Esther was an orphan; she had no mother or father. Esther was a stranger; she had been taken into exile. Esther was an outcast; she lived with her cousin, Mordecai, inside the palace gates. These relationships that define Esther aren't the warm and fuzzy kind. Hallmark doesn't have a card for orphans, strangers, or outcasts.

Perhaps you know what it is to be orphaned, whether by parents who are gone, abusive, self-absorbed, or negligent. Perhaps you feel orphaned because your parents or other family members misunderstand or judge you. Whether we are four, fourteen, or forty, we never stop feeling the humiliating ache of being without parents. In her heartbreaking novel *White Oleander*, Janet Fitch poignantly describes the longing for a mother that can leave us feeling desperate when we are without. She writes about the cries heard in a hospital maternity ward: "All down the ward, they called for their mothers. *Mommy, ma, mom, mama*. Even with husbands at their sides, they called for mama.... A grown woman sobbing like a child. *Mommy* ... But then I realized, they did not [necessarily] mean their own mothers. They wanted the real mother ... mother of a fierce compassion, a woman large enough to hold all the pain, to carry it away ... mothers who would breathe for us when we could not breathe anymore, who would fight for us, who would kill for us, die for us."[1]

I understand these cries for a mother. Just this week I came down with a severe case of bronchitis, and all I wanted was for my mom to come and take care of me. When we can't call on our mothers in times of distress or need, we experience the ache of being orphaned.

Maybe you know what it is to be a stranger. Instead of feeling like the beautiful, hope-filled, strange women described in the previous chapter, you feel alone in the middle of a packed church or alone in your struggles with your finances, your addiction, or your difficult marriage. Or you feel strange because you drive a car that was made ten years ago, work at the mall instead of a fancy office, or don't fit in with a small group at church. Maybe you don't pray anymore or you doubt God; that can make you feel strange. In the midst of our loneliness, the longing to belong often taunts us that something must be wrong with us, something strange, something that keeps us from experiencing the relational life that we imagine everyone else has but often seems out of our grasp.

Do you know what it's like to be an outcast? My friend Rachel writes about her experience of being outcast.

I was almost eight months pregnant at my high school graduation (who knew a graduation gown doubled as a maternity dress?), but by then, baby cribs, layette gowns, and *The Womanly Art of Breastfeeding* (this is the title of a real book?) had pushed aside college scholarships, graduation parties, a semester abroad, and the last summer after high school spent in anticipation of going off to college. I was eventually able to go to a local college because my parents helped me with my new baby, while I lived in their basement. A relative actually suggested to my parents that if they were going to "let" me move back in with them (after running off to try to make a life with my baby's father), that I shouldn't be allowed to come upstairs and out of the basement unless it was an emergency. I started wondering if I was in some "exception" category to those that God mercifully loved. Most churches I tried wanted to shoehorn me into a specific area. I tried the single groups only to feel like a freak because I was hanging around unmarried people who were in their forties. I tried parenting/mothering groups only to feel like a freak because I didn't have a husband, a minivan, acrylic nails, and a myriad of other mysteries I didn't understand. I passed out fliers at my church, expressing interest in starting a playgroup/mom group for anyone who wanted to take part, and I got a call from the pastor's wife explaining that there were very few appropriate times for such a group to meet, as most of the mothers in the church had husbands, and family time was very important to them. I couldn't be expected to understand these things. Usually, the word "freak" is applied to people that our culture has marginalized—those who may wear Goth makeup, are into strange hobbies or practices, or are all-around crazy. But as a middle-class, Caucasian, eighteen-year-old mother, I felt like the word fit perfectly. Nobody was telling me that God still loved me.[2]

Feeling like an outcast, whether because of our own choices or the judgments of others, can leave us feeling pretty unlovable and wondering about our place in the world.

All women are misfits. We do not fit into this world without amputations.

—Marge Piercy

"Those People"

Back to Esther—the orphan, stranger, and outcast. The humiliating realities of Esther's relational life become the platform for her unfolding story. Three other characters shape the plot. The first is Mordecai, Esther's cousin. He is a kind and faithful man who surely watched prayerfully as Esther was ordered to the palace "beauty contest" to be evaluated by the king. During this beauty contest, Esther meets the second character: King Xerxes. Esther finds favors with the king, which eventually gives her a position of influence with him. The third character is King Xerxes' wicked aide, Haman. Haman hatches a plot to kill the Jews, and Esther is a Jew. When Haman presents his murderous scheme to the king, he justifies the nasty scheme by describing the people he would murder as "an odd set of people scattered through the provinces ... who don't fit in" (Est. 3:8).

Initially, the king agrees. "'Go ahead,' the king said to Haman, '... do whatever you want with *those people*'" (Est. 3:11, italics added).

At Haman's request, "Bulletins were sent out by couriers to all the king's provinces with orders to massacre, kill, and eliminate" *those people* (Est. 3:13). Esther's humiliation as an orphan, stranger, and outcast made her vulnerable to Haman's plot. The unfolding story reveals something about Haman's heart, Esther's heart, and God's heart. Haman's dark heart moved him to use violence to get rid of evidence and reminders of God in the world (the Jews were God's chosen people). Esther's courageous heart compelled her to risk her own life when she eventually revealed to the king that if Haman's plot was to be carried out, she would be killed. She didn't have any way of knowing whether the king would have compassion on her and save her people or side with Haman. We see God's redeeming heart as he uses a young, orphaned woman to expose evil and fight for good. This seems to be the story that God wants to tell over and over again: he gives strength to the weak, rescue to the needy, and victory to the downtrodden.

The humiliation of being weak, needy, and downtrodden becomes the context for salvation.

After all, the themes of humiliation in the midst of relational realties are clearly seen in the story of God's own Son. God entered this world as a helpless baby without a place to lay his head (Luke 2: 6–7; 9:58), as a stranger who came unto his own but they received him not (John 1:11), and as an outcast who walked up a lonely hill outside the palace gates to a place called Golgotha (Matt. 27:32–44). When we see Jesus' humiliation as an impoverished stranger and outcast, it will not surprise us that those experiences are what enable him to align himself with the last and the least, *those people*. The apostle James went so far as to write, "[God] chose the world's down-and-out as the kingdom's first citizens" (James 2:5). Esther's status as an orphan, stranger, and outcast put her in the perfect circumstances to live out God's story. Her unfolding saga confirms that God's plan for "those people" is to care for, protect, and rescue them. Consider for a moment the times when you've felt orphaned, strange, or outcast. Did you experience "the fellowship of sharing in [Jesus'] sufferings" (Phil. 3:10 NIV), knowing that his humiliating circumstances set the context for the salvation story? Or did you feel cut off from God because of your humiliation? Do you resist categorizing yourself as one of "those people"?

Those people: the losers, the fools, the uncool. The unwed mother. The nineteen-year-old orphan in Phnom Penh who prostitutes herself to buy rice for her mother and six brothers and sister. The woman so addicted to alcohol that she exchanges all of her children, giving up her parental rights, for a twelve-pack of Michelob Light a day. The woman from one of the richest neighborhoods in America spending the night in jail on charges of domestic violence. The divorced, the wealthy, environmentalists, AIDS patients, Democrats,

Republicans, legalists, universalists, addicts—the orphans, strangers, and outcasts. We're really all poor and needy, "the least of these."

Esther's heart for "those people" came from being one of them and beautifully reveals God's heart, a heart that is ultimately revealed in Jesus, another impoverished stranger and outcast. Humiliation in relationships allows us to know something about a God who willingly humbled himself to be with us. Counselor and author Dan Allender describes the relationships that grow out of humiliation: "Some of our stories describe abandonment, betrayal, and ambivalence. We experience these losses and assaults as orphans, strangers, and widows. Should it surprise us then that God wants to make himself known as the Father who protects the orphans, as the Brother who encourages the stranger, and as the Lover who cherishes the widow? The Triune God who is One wants to redeem our story and restore with his love what our story took from us."[3]

Humiliating circumstances can compel us to bring our relational wounds to God. His wounds for the sake of relationship with us, suffered by his Son on the cross, heal our wounds. I don't know about you, but scarred hands are the only ones that I want to cling to in the pain of relationships. When we have been healed by Christ's wounds, we then can go to others who are wounded, take their hands, and walk with them in the way of healing. Esther's humiliation as an orphan, stranger, and outcast compelled her to align herself with other orphans, strangers, and outcasts. Esther models for us how we can live authentically and purposefully in the midst of relational pain. She emerges from the shadows to rescue her people in unlikely and risky ways. First, Esther comes just as she is, without pretense or shame. Her humiliating circumstances allow her to let go of looking good and live in genuine humility, with nothing to protect or prove. Second, Esther remains committed to a purpose: to love others, no matter what the cost. She could have kept quiet and not told the king that she is one of the people Haman intends to kill, but she values honoring and serving others more than prestige or power.

The Résumé of the Heart

Before Esther made public her experience as an orphan, a stranger, and an outcast, and before she aligned herself with "those people," Esther was summoned to a beauty contest to be held before the king. She was given beauty treatments, fed special food, assigned seven personal maids, and given the best room in the palace. She completed twelve months of beauty treatments and put together a résumé that was unparalleled among the women of her time. When the day of the pageant arrived, each young woman was told that she could take whatever she wanted with her to impress the king. What would you have taken? Accessories, a special outfit, a list of your credentials? Certainly that $95 melt-away magic undergarment!

Esther asked for nothing.

"Esther, just as she was, won the admiration of everyone who saw her" (Est. 2:15).

Just as she was. That takes courage. No mask, no false self, no accomplishments, no shame or failures, no melt-away magic undergarment. What's left? Or should I ask, *Who* is left? Esther is the only book in the Bible that does not mention God, yet it profoundly reveals the heart of God, because he isn't hidden by a human résumé.

Humiliation becomes humility when I believe that I can look bad *because* I am in the presence of Love. Esther had no guarantee that the king would choose her. In fact, if she was not chosen, she would be relegated to live in the palace as a "kept woman," not free to marry and obligated to be available for whatever the king might order. Esther had every reason to cover up her flaws, hide her humiliating credentials, and pretend to be somebody. It takes courage to live authentically, and it takes bravery of heroic proportions not to hide. Esther could come as she was before the king only because she knew, heart and soul, that there was a greater King, whose promise she surely heard from her cousin Mordecai as he taught her the Scriptures: "Hear, O Israel: The LORD our God, the LORD is one. Love the LORD your God with all your heart and with all your soul and with all your strength.... Fear the LORD your God, serve him only and take your oaths in his name.... The LORD commanded us to obey all these decrees and to fear the LORD our God, so that we might always prosper and be kept alive" (Deut. 6:4, 5, 13, 24 NIV).

With no guarantee of reward, Esther chose to be authentic rather than to cover up the truths of her life. In making this choice, she set the stage for a decision that would soon require her to risk everything for the sake of her true King.

Coming as we are, in humility and authenticity, is a necessary practice that will lead us into a life of dependence on God and a certainty about his calling on our lives. We often get this backward. We believe that we must make our lives look good to fit his calling rather than believing that all the parts of our lives—the good and the bad, our successes and failures, our joys and heartbreaks—are part of our preparation for our calling. We believe that we can't

> *Only to your lover do you expose your worst. [Understanding] the Gospel results in the most generous, secure, adventurous expression of the human heart. It risks the certainty of being acceptable and accepted.*
>
> —Sebastian Moore,
> *This Crucified Jesus Is No Stranger*

look bad because we don't believe that we are really in the presence of great Love, the love that transforms our humiliation into humility so that we can be of service to our King.

I don't personally know any modern-day Esthers—women who hold the fate of an entire nation in their hands. But I do know one woman named Gigi, who, with no guarantee of reward, made the same choice Esther did: she chose to be authentic and refused to cover up the truth of her difficult life.

When I met Gigi four years ago, her six-month marriage had just fallen apart. Gigi explained to me how she had diligently sought God's guidance in her dating life and in her decision to marry. Because Gigi was an orphan, she relied on her pastor and others in her church to help her in the important decisions she was making about her future. She knew that God had called her to a path of service, which she believed would include a ministry in the areas of social justice and racial reconciliation. To further her preparation for God's call on her life, she planned to begin seminary just a few months after her marriage.

When Gigi's husband told her he wanted a divorce, he didn't really explain his reasons for wanting out of the marriage. Gigi later learned that he had a secret life that their marriage threatened, and he decided that he didn't want to live torn between two worlds anymore. He chose a world without Gigi. When Gigi came to my counseling office, she was humiliated. She had prayed, tried to obey, sought counsel, and now this already orphaned girl was outcast and certainly feeling like a stranger—a young woman in seminary, already divorced, wanting to serve God, and wondering how in the world that would ever happen.

For months, Gigi and I grieved together over her lost marriage, her confusion, and her anger at a God who seemed to have abandoned her. Gigi questioned her calling and wondered who would ever want her in ministry with her humiliating credentials. Yet Gigi continued on in seminary. She often worked three jobs to pay her bills. She spent many lonely nights crying out to God about her excruciating circumstances.

Two years after her divorce, Gigi began to think about dating again. She wondered who would want an orphan, stranger, and outcast. She remained steadfast in her sense of calling to ministry and longed for a husband who would share her vision. She often asked me, "Sharon, do you think my expectations are too high? Do you think there's someone like this out there? Do you think he'd want me?" My answer was always the same: "I don't know. He would have to be a gift from God."

When we are in the valley of humiliation, it's hard to believe that God will give us good gifts. Over the months after her shattering divorce, Gigi became a woman of great courage. She told the truth about her life. She didn't hide her confusion or anger. She didn't stop wanting good things. She struggled to obey God in the absence of any reward. She didn't know it, but she was becoming a woman who was ready for a calling far beyond her meager human imaginings.

One year ago, Gigi packed her bags for South Africa to complete an internship required for her seminary degree. She interviewed with several mission organizations and was honest about her journey and her sense of calling to a ministry of social justice and racial reconciliation. Several missions turned her down. One mission accepted her, but then Gigi was unable to raise the necessary funds for the internship. During our counseling session one week, Gigi asked a question that I couldn't answer: "Sharon, why would God make me for things I can't have? Here I am divorced. I almost have a completed seminary degree that it looks like I won't be able to use. I am lonely. I don't have any money. What is God doing?"

I did not have a warm and fuzzy answer for Gigi, but I did remind her of the story of Esther. We talked about Esther's seeming limitations as an orphan, stranger, and outcast and how God used her when she refused to hide. A few weeks later, Gigi learned that she had been accepted by a mission that would help her with her financial needs. She set off for South Africa—an orphan, stranger, and outcast—trusting that God would use her. Gigi didn't know that God had a set a plan in motion for her, much as he did for Esther, that would not be limited by shattered dreams or human schemes.

> *Danger*
>
> *The world is full of danger*
>
> *But if I never try to go outside*
>
> *My heart will waste away*
>
> —JJ Heller, "Save Me"

The Resolve of a Braveheart

Esther aligned herself with "those people"—the orphans, strangers, and outcasts. She prepared to represent God's heart by coming just as she was, which allowed her to do the work of the kingdom with a resolve of heroic proportions.

You remember the story. King Xerxes chose Esther in the beauty pageant. She became queen of the land. She escaped her humiliating circumstances! Then she learned of the plight of "those people"—her people. She bravely went before the king uninvited, just as she was, and she told the truth. Esther's courage cannot be underestimated in this bold move—to go before the king uninvited could result in an immediate death sentence. She explained to the king, "I am one of those people your aide Haman has scheduled to kill." She risked everything that she had gained. If the king rejected her request, he could remove her as queen. When he learned that she was one of "those people," he could sentence her to death as well.

Esther took this courageous action after Mordecai reminded her, "If you persist in staying silent at a time like this, help and deliverance will arrive for [those people] from someplace else; but you and your family will be wiped out. Who knows? Maybe you were made queen for just such a time as this" (Est. 4:14).

Esther agreed to approach the king and tell him the truth, saying, "If I die, I die" (Est. 4:16).

Esther's resolve began in her humiliating realities. It grew as she first stood before the king without pretense or cover-up. And it became the turning point in the salvation of an entire nation when Esther surrendered, believing that everything that she had experienced was to prepare her for a time like this. Esther risked losing the favor of this earthly king because she knew that the only favor that matters is the favor of the King. Her life reveals that finding favor with God means sharing in his suffering.

Our humiliating relational realities allow us to share in the suffering of Jesus. They prepare us for our calling to minister to other humiliated people. And best of all, they allow us to know a love that is not based on a résumé—a love that is limitless, that never forgets who we are, that keeps believing in who we can be, that holds our hands when we are afraid, uncertain, or filled with anticipation—the love of Jesus, who loves us when we are good for nothing because it is his love alone that makes us ready for something!

I saw Gigi again this week for the first time since her year in South Africa. She called for an appointment and told me that she would be bringing someone with her. I had received emails from her throughout the year about her work in a church in Soweto, South Africa. She wrote about the complicated racial realities and the need for a way to minister in love in the midst of a lot of hurt, hatred, and violence. I prayed often for Gigi's safety, although I suspected that God was up to more than just keeping her safe.

I greeted Gigi at my front door and immediately noted the man by her side. He was an elegant man with eyes that held such sorrow and strength that I was a bit taken back upon first meeting him. Gigi introduced Sihle and told me he was the pastor of the church in Soweto, where she ministered in her internship. Sihle had grown up in Soweto and had experienced the absence of a father, poverty, and violence, as was true of so many of his countrymen. His path had taken a strange turn when he came to know Christ and attended Bible college. His education eventually led him out of Soweto to seminary, but he could never get away from a sense of God's calling on his life to return to his town and minister out of what he knew of God and how God's message intersected with matters of social justice and racial reconciliation.

As Gigi and Sihle ministered together, talked about their callings, and grew to know one another better, it became clear that these two orphans, strangers, and outcasts were made for a time such as this. Gigi shared with me that they planned to be married and return to Soweto to minister together.

I could see clearly how Gigi's humiliating experiences as an orphan, stranger, and outcast had uniquely prepared her for the life that God had been planning all along. Gigi and Sihle's story is not a fairy tale with a "happily ever after" ending. They will return to a place of violence, misunderstanding, and potential prejudice. They will minister in the midst of great suffering in the hope of bringing good news about the favor of God, favor that does not always bring a warm and fuzzy life but that does bring a relationship with a God who uses humiliating human realities to bring us to a resting place in a love that cannot be earned and can never be lost.

"Oh Sharon," Gigi grabbed my arm as she was going out the door. "Do you remember all those times when I asked you if you thought I wanted too much and if there would ever be someone for me?" I remembered. I have wondered about that question not only for Gigi but for myself and for countless others. I recalled that I had told Gigi that the man she wanted would have to be a gift from God and had often thought to myself, "But God's gifts are confusing or can seem a long time in coming!"

What Gigi told me next is something I will never forget. Her story reminds me that God's good gifts come in the midst of our humiliating realities. His good gifts come because we don't hide from those realities but rather surrender them to his love, and in the process, we discover our calling—a calling that grows not out of who we are but out of how we are loved.

"Sharon," Gigi continued with a sparkle in her eye, "Sihle's name means 'a gift from God'!"

Just for You

1. Look through old photographs of yourself and recall times when you felt like an orphan, stranger, or outcast. How did you respond to those realities—in shame, service, anger, or faith?

2. What do the relationships you seek out reveal about how you perceive yourself? For example, do you scramble to be in the "inner circle" at your church or work? Do you offer care to those who are seemingly less important?

3. Describe a time when you felt safe enough to look bad because you were confident you were in the presence of love. What was it that made you feel safe enough to let your guard down?

4. Has there been a time when you felt God was calling you to love others, even at a cost to yourself? How did you experience fellowship with him during this time? If you haven't experienced a sense of calling, consider praying daily to ask God to help you understand your calling.

5. How does knowing you are loved unconditionally by God allow you to take risks in relationships? What risks have you taken to love others?

CHAPTER FIVE

The Desert of Estrangement

Every crucifixion contains certain characteristics common to all crucifixions: Rejection, Pain, Unfairness, Rumor, Innuendoes, More pain, Misunderstanding, Demeaning, Belittling, Loss of reputation, Loss of friends. Often, there is excommunication. The loss of *all* things.

—Gene Edwards, *Exquisite Agony*

THIS IS THE CHAPTER I didn't want to write. The dictionary defines *estrangement* as "alienation." Alienation in relationships leaves us dazed, hurt, and confused. I have known alienation in a marriage, a relationship in which promises were exchanged that I thought were a guarantee but that I discovered could be broken into pieces that continue to cut and wound. I have known alienation in a friendship, when frequent telephone calls were exchanged for silence, and shared memories faded into the heartbreak of absence. I have known alienation from a church, when different beliefs and philosophies carved a canyon that even long-standing friendships could not bridge. And most recently I have known alienation from my daughter, a child who came from me, into whom I poured myself and who, for one year, stepped away from our relationship to find herself.

I didn't know if I could write about estrangement because the recent experience with my daughter was so painful that I frequently awoke each morning with unbidden tears on my face. I have battled shame over the distance in this relationship that was once so close. At times, the pain was so intense I refused to talk about it, certain that doing so would open a Pandora's box of suffering that I would not be able to contain.

This part of my story is not a happy one, I know. But I share it here because something was about to occur on that bathroom floor that would change forever the progression of my life. . . . What happened was that I started to pray.

—Elizabeth Gilbert, *Eat, Pray, Love*

I raged, wept, tried to escape, and grieved. In this desperate state of relationship, I also discovered grace that knocked me flat on my face before God.

When we can't bear the pain and we can't solve the problem, either we can die in bitterness and resentment or we can choose life, knowing that it must be a Life outside of ourselves because estrangement becomes a desert within that dries up any efforts to create life by ourselves. That is the gift of estrangement: it compels us to the Life outside of ourselves because it causes us to reach the end of all of our resources. We stop asking God to take our side and simply ask him to take over.

During the year of estrangement from Kristin, I discovered

a few practices that kept me from falling into the abyss of hopelessness. Throughout this chapter, I will share with you some thoughts on what to do when you don't know what to do, because there is nothing like estrangement in our relationships for leaving us feeling helpless. These are not tactics to help you get the relationship back or to make everything work. These are simply practices that have kept me on the healing path, enabled me to maintain my sanity, and helped me to remain focused on life rather than death.

The Gift of Estrangement

Estrangement is another one of those gifts that we would never choose, and usually it takes a while for us to see that it really is a gift, maybe even the most valuable gift. Our usual reaction to estrangement is to become defensive and assign blame. The harshness of this reality first compels us to sort out who is right and who is wrong in the breach in relationship. But if we stay stuck in the blame game, we won't receive the gift of estrangement. When we stop trying to understand who is right and who is wrong, the inexplicable realities of estrangement can draw us to the truth that what we are experiencing is actually a crucifixion; something is being put to death. Estrangement becomes a gift when we realize that the "something" that is dying is not the relationship but rather the patterns or beliefs within us that need to die to make room for new life.

The Blame Game

Whenever a breach in human relationships occurs, we want to figure out who is to blame. Somehow we feel better if we can pick a side and clearly declare who is good and who is bad. Whenever a relational breakdown occurs, both parties always contribute to the failure, but our need to be in the right often keeps us from experiencing the healing gifts that come in broken relationships. It may be necessary to dissect who is at fault, but we step onto the path of healing only when we focus on the "plank in our own eye" rather than on the "speck" in someone else's (Luke 6:42 NIV).

Estrangement forces us to confront ourselves and consider how we have been careless, have sinned, or have neglected a relationship. Most of us stop there. We identify either how we have been wronged or how we have wronged others, then we collapse under the weight of bitterness or self-hatred. Self-awareness is not an end in itself. We are on the path of transformation when our self-awareness takes us out of ourselves. I have learned that when I begin to feel the weight of my own sin or failure, I don't have to carry that weight alone. Whenever I recall moments in a relationship when I or others have failed, I confess that moment to God. My confession of a painful moment allows me to connect with God so that I am not alone with my sorrow. It also provides an opportunity for me to apologize to God for my own sin, foolishness, or failure. This confession enables me to step off the mental merry-go-round of blame and hurt and to keep my heart open to God. Confession also creates a willingness to acknowledge the harm I have done to others and a continued willingness to make amends for those harms, if appropriate.

Have you had experiences in relationships that haunt you? Do you have conversations with yourself about things that you'd like to say to others if you got the chance? Whenever those thoughts come, take a few minutes to confess them to God. For example, if you are troubled by your own failures and the harm you've done others, you can say something like, "God, I apologize for being careless and hurting my friend. I am willing to make amends for the harm I've done. Show me the way to do this." If you are bombarded by thoughts about times when others have hurt you, confess that as well, saying, "God, I can't stop thinking about the time that my husband lied to me. Release me from the bondage of my own thoughts."

A Crucifixion

Confession can keep us going, but it doesn't change the reality of a broken relationship. Estrangement is shattering. Few realities affect our lives more profoundly or painfully. The break in a relationship often contains accusations, judgments, and misunderstandings. It pierces us to our core and truly feels like we are being crucified—hung out to die, publicly humiliated, naked, ashamed, and alone. I am intrigued by the words of author Gene Edwards about the painful yet hopeful realities of crucifixion in relationships: "There is no limit to the effect a crucifixion can have on your life. It could possibly leave you lame for the rest of your life, its destructive power following you throughout your life and on to your grave. On the other hand, it *can* affect you positively—so positively that when you re-emerge, you are almost a totally different person."[1]

A crucifixion? That doesn't seem too extreme if you have experienced the painful realities of an estranged relationship. This past Mother's Day I checked my mailbox twice, hoping that a card somehow found its way there from my daughter. I carried my cell phone with me throughout the day, certain that she would call. I imagined a scene of reconciliation and brushed away frustrated tears as I drove by myself to church. I watched all the other mothers with their families in church and felt like a monster-mother who could not prove her worth by having a beaming family at her side. I stopped at Dairy Queen on the way home, determined to lose myself in an M&M's Blizzard, only to find myself choking on the ice cream because it could not take away the bitter loss of relationship.

Although I knew that both my daughter and I contributed to the break in our relationship, it felt like a crucifixion—something done to me that felt vicious, inhumane, and unjust beyond belief. I could feel the nails tearing through my flesh, ripping at my hands and feet, and shredding my soul. At times, it felt like it would destroy me.

If relational breakdowns feel like crucifixions, we would do well to consider the source of crucifixions. Beyond our placing blame, confessing our failures, and feeling the inexplicable pain of the broken relationship, could it be that there is a Power greater than us at work even in the complete failure of a relationship? Edwards explains that when we are crucified by failed human relationships, we enter into Christ's crucifixion.[2] He writes, "Refusal to accept your crucifixion as wholly from the hand of God only means you were not crucified, you were just mistreated. Only when you accept that it came from God, only then is it a *true* crucifixion ... from the hand of God, and God alone."[3]

I have surrendered hundreds of times to God's purposes in the midst of a crucifixion I would have never asked for. Whether it was a broken marriage, a distant friend, or a chasm between me and my daughter, I often could not find the words to express all that I was feeling. This prayer from Gene Edwards has helped me immensely and given me words of surrender when I could not find them for myself: "It is from you, my Lord! For my good! This thing is wholly between you and me. There are no others involved in this bloody hour. I do not like this; it is the most difficult thing ever to enter my life. But it is you. I now call you Lord, sovereign Lord. Others meant it to me for evil; Lord, you meant it for good! I accept this crucifixion! From you!"[4]

As I begin to confess my sin, feel the pain of my broken relationships, and believe that God could be the beginning and the ending of these painful chapters in my story, I start to experience peace. I become willing to consider that God might redeem this awful reality for good. That gives me hope that estrangement is not the final word in my relationships. But I need to be honest: most days I still battle with anger, resentment, blame, defending myself, nurturing a grudge, and even thinking about some form of retaliation. Embracing crucifixion has not come naturally to me at all, but my dark, brooding thoughts about this broken relationship with my daughter began to reveal to me why a crucifixion might be necessary.

Don't be afraid. . . . Don't you see, you planned evil against me but God used those same plans for my good.

—Genesis 50:19–20

If you are feeling the pain of a crucifixion due to a relational breakdown, I encourage you to take the prayer suggested by Edwards and personalize it. Add descriptors of your own loss and pain and ask for the grace to accept this from God. Something begins to shift in our hearts and makes room for peace when we stop focusing on the harm the other person is doing to us and begin looking for how God might use this harm for good.

The Purpose of Estrangement

The purpose of any crucifixion is to destroy. Christ was crucified to destroy the power of sin and death. Estrangement in relationships certainly makes destruction real; we feel the disintegration at a cellular level. The Old Testament refers to forming a covenant of relationship as "cutting a covenant." Ancient people formed a covenant by slaughtering an animal, such as a lamb. They then cut the animal in half, laid the two halves on the ground, and walked between the halves saying,

"May it be done to me as it was done to this animal if I break the covenant." Having been through a divorce, I can tell you that breaking the covenant of marriage feels very much like taking a live animal and ripping it in half. Crawling through the desert of estrangement, I have certainly felt the destruction and asked, "Why me? What good is there in this for me? Why my crucifixion?"

Destroying Sin

When we embrace crucifixion as something God purposes for good, we allow for the possibility that our destruction may lead us upward. Our hearts turn away from ourselves, away from the confusing pain in the relationship, and toward God. When our need to be right, our fury to force things to work, and our craving for affirmation is destroyed, we are free. The freedom of living with nothing to prove and nothing to protect comes only when we surrender to a death of self. Surrendering to a death of myself means that I exchange my agenda for the relationship for an openness to how God might be using this pain to transform me. Surrender means I exchange my need to defend myself for a desire to grow. Surrender means I exchange my anger at injustice for sorrow that human relationships hurt. Surrender means that I exchange making this estrangement "the point" in my life for gratitude that it is drawing me closer to Christ. Estrangement in relationships accomplishes divine purposes when I allow it to destroy anything that keeps me on the treadmill of proving and protecting.

I can still clearly recall a moment of surrender in my estrangement from my daughter. I was sitting on an airplane, brooding about the injustice and pain in our relationship. My heart was full of defensiveness and confusion about how anything good could come from this. I felt as if everything good

I had contributed to our relationship was fading away, and I was frantic to somehow remind Kristin of all that she was losing. As I started to pray, I felt the Holy Spirit nudge me, "Can you let go?" A little angrily, I thought, "What choice do I have?" Tears began to well up in my eyes as I acknowledged how exhausted I was from defending myself, propping up my ego, rehearsing Kristin's wrongs and my rights, and suppressing some of my own failures in our relationship. I realized that I could continue to be in a tug-of-war with God over this, or I could let go—let go of my pride, my ego, my righteousness, and my failures. I felt my shoulders relax as I surrendered, and I heard the Holy Spirit commune with my spirit: "She'll come back to you when both of you are in a place to renew the relationship. Now is the time for you to surrender all the good and bad that you've contributed to this relationship and let me sort it out."

If you are experiencing a broken relationship, take some time to acknowledge all that is stirring in your heart. As you examine the hurt, pride, defensiveness, outrage, bitterness, and shame, ask yourself what you would like to be true of you whether or not the relationship is ever healed. Would you like to exchange hurt for compassion, pride for humility, defensiveness for wisdom, outrage for discernment, bitterness for joy, and shame for peace? Make a list of what is stirring in your heart as well as what you'd like to be true of you. Consider thanking God for this difficult time and surrendering specific

> *God knew what he was doing from the very beginning. He decided from the outset to shape the lives of those who love him along the same lines as the life of his Son. The Son stands first in the line of humanity he restored.*
>
> —Romans 8:29

emotional responses to him. For example, "I surrender my defensiveness about this. As I drop my guard, will you give me wisdom to see the truth about myself and others?" Ask God to take the estrangement and all that it brings up in you and exchange it for a transformative experience.

Exposing Darkness to Light

In the year of estrangement from my daughter, I discovered a darkness within myself that needed to be brought to the light. The estrangement brought to light the dark desire for my children to validate my worth and affirm me. It's a dark desire because I know my true worth is found only in relationship with the Crucified One. The estrangement revealed hidden motives and taught me again that when I surrender my own agenda, I can trust that God is at work fulfilling his purposes. The estrangement revealed weaknesses I needed to confess to God and others. An experience of painful estrangement—a crucifixion—exposes my desire to avoid suffering, my determination to never lose, and my furious defense that I must be right. The first step that takes us out of these dark places is to embrace the very things we are resisting. In other words, estrangement is an opportunity to surrender to suffering, to become willing to lose, and to allow our wisdom to be replaced by a greater wisdom.

Surrender to Suffering

Can you imagine a life without suffering? That's what we often conclude we want, but suffering can actually be a path to healing. When we do not have a redemptive attitude toward crucifixion, we miss the potential healing that comes in the midst of brokenness. The stereotypical bitter, resentful woman is one who simply believes that the heartache in her relationships is just a series of ugly incidents taking place between ugly people. As Edwards points out in his beautiful book on crucifixion in relationships, "A redemptive attitude is the only *safe* attitude to have, when one is hanging on a cross."[5] When we embrace suffering, we believe that it will transform us into more than we were before. An escape from pain is also an escape from change.

During a recent trip to Israel, I had the privilege of visiting Yad Vashem, Israel's unforgettable memorial to the six million Jews who were killed in the Holocaust. I spent several hours in one exhibit titled "Spots of Light: To Be a Woman in the Holocaust." This exhibit featured a film with different women talking about their experiences in the prison camps. The film was breathtaking in its beauty and simplicity and heartstopping as its narrators told their stories of unthinkable suffering. Woman after woman told of forced estrangement from family, friends, and home. This is how one woman summed up her experience: "We all wanted revenge, and we learned that the best revenge against suffering was to try to develop a spiritual life."[6]

Since my time in Israel, I have thought about this woman's response to suffering and what it means to develop a spiritual life. For the women in the prison camps, a spiritual life was not dependent on physical, emotional, or even spiritual resources, because they were certainly deprived of all three. We tend to believe that we can develop a spiritual life when we can get away to a retreat center, feel emotionally connected to our community, or be led by a pastor or worship leader. The women in this film challenge us with the idea that a spiritual life is developed when we choose to see more than the material. We can choose to look beyond the hurt and injustice in relationships to see God sitting with us in the pain, allowing it to refine us into women who are not bound to earth but are turned toward heaven.

In the face of unspeakable suffering, I can blame, argue, kick, and scream, or I can look for something more. I can accept responsibility for my part in the relational breakdown, confess the realities of my heart, and surrender to God. I stop wanting the other person to change, and I long for my own transformation so much that I give thanks for this estrangement because of all that it has revealed that I would not have seen otherwise. We are on the path of healing, even in the desert of estrangement, not when the suffering stops but when we believe that God is destroying what is seen in order to produce what is unseen. The apostle Paul says it this way, "So we're not giving up. How could we! Even though on the outside it often looks like things are falling apart on us, on the inside, where God is making new life, not a day goes by without his unfolding grace.... There's far more here than meets the eye. The things we see now are here today, gone tomorrow. But the things we can't see now will last forever" (2 Cor. 4:16, 18).

> *Pain removes the veil; it plants the flag of truth within the fortress of a rebel soul.*
>
> —C. S. Lewis,
> *The Problem of Pain*

It takes intentionality to see that there is far more here than a broken relationship. Take note of the things that are becoming true of you that would not be true without the difficulties of this broken relationship. Do you pray more? Have you reached out to other friends who have given you support during this time? Are you more compassionate for others in estranged relationships? As you note God's transformative work in your life, you will be able to give thanks for the estranged relationship, because it is evidence that God in his mercy uses everything—even, and maybe especially, broken relationships—to change us.

During the time that I was estranged from my daughter, I confided in a dear older friend named Julia. A few months ago, Julia was diagnosed with ovarian cancer and given less than a year to live. I recently spent the afternoon with her, sitting on her bed beside her, watching her sleep, and waiting for a few moments of wakefulness to talk with her. While I was there, she asked if I would massage her back. "It has been so long since someone touched me," she said.

As I tenderly massaged her back, I thought about her life. Her husband had died only months ago. She lived on a fixed income. I don't remember her ever taking a vacation or talking about going on a shopping spree. She was estranged from her adult son. She'd had a radical double mastectomy long before the days of reconstructive surgery. Yet all of this suffering had not left Julia bitter or resentful. She is a woman full of faith, compassion, understanding, and kindness. I cannot think of a woman I trust more. Julia's suffering has drawn many women to her over the years. Something about just being with her is healing. She is a living example to me of someone who chose to develop a spiritual life in response to her suffering. Julia never complains, doesn't hold any grudges, and does not see herself as a victim. Her serenity is evidence that she has spent a lot of time talking to Jesus about her suffering and that she has accepted a relationship with him as the answer to all her questions. As I saw the beauty of suffering in her life, I prayed that God would give me the courage to see all that he longed to grow in my own life in response to suffering.

Become Willing to Lose

The way of crucifixion looks like the way of failure. When we experience estrangement in relationships, it is natural to feel shame, because we are losing. I can accept losing when I understand how God wins. *God wins by losing.* He wisely and tenderly uses the brokenness in our relationships to make us into his image. This is what Jesus taught: the first will be last and the last will be first; the meek will inherit (not conquer) the earth; you must lose your life to find it. Richard Rohr writes, "Jesus is a person and at the same time a process, Jesus is the Son of God, but at the same time he is 'the Way.' He's the goal, but he's also the means, and the means is always the way of the cross."[7] Estrangement in relationships can be the process that allows us to lose ourselves and become like Jesus.

When we reach the end of our human resources, when there is nothing that we can do, when what we want most is out of our grasp, and when we are relationally impoverished, we have the opportunity to be radically dependent on God. I wince with embarrassment as I think about my energetic, determined, strong-willed, younger self. I recall teaching my daughter, "Kristin, there is no situation that you can't do something about. You can always do something!" Ironically, it was the estrangement in my relationship with her that taught me that there are some situations in which I am powerless, in which there is nothing I can do. I can either rail against these realities or become willing to lose, believing that what feels like death may actually bring new life.

> *The way to love anything is to realize that it might be lost.*
>
> —G. K. Chesterton, *Common Sense 101*

During my estrangement from Kristin, there were many times I needed to confess my poverty to God—my complete lack of resources, ideas, and energy to make things work. I prayed, "God, my daughter and our relationship is in your hands." I was reminded of Jesus' crucifixion, when he surrendered to being estranged from his Father so that we would never have to experience that most terrible alienation—alienation from God. Jesus expressed the anguish of his estrangement, "My God, my God, why have you forsaken me?" (Matt. 27:46 NIV); and then modeled the transforming surrender we can experience in the midst of estrangement, "Father, into your hands I commit my spirit" (Luke 23:46 NIV). Surrender allows us to keep our wounds open so that we can receive Christ in us.

Express your anguish to God in detail; don't hold back anything. Then follow the way of Jesus by praying, "Father, this relationship is in your hands." When we give up the need to win, the need to be right, the need to make everything work, and the need to be loved, we can let go of ourselves. We aren't really free until we're free from ourselves. Estrangement in relationships is perhaps the most painful gift, but it allows us to get ourselves out of the way so that we can welcome Christ.

Exchange My Judgment for a Greater Judgment

Yesterday I had coffee with someone whom I had not seen for over thirteen years. In fact, he was ten years old when I last saw him. His parents were dear friends. We ministered in church together, ate many meals together, and often swapped babysitting. This now twenty-three-year-old reminded me that I used to give him Pop-Tarts for breakfast! Our families became estranged due to many reasons, a lot of them having to do with the different judgments we made about ourselves, about each other, and about God. My conversation with this young man as I was in the midst of writing about estrangement in relationships reminded me that I've made a lot of ridiculous judgments in my life.

I have judged myself to be the one who really needed to save myself, from my emptiness, my loneliness, and my sinfulness. I have ended up more empty, more lonely, and more mired in a willful attempt to control my life, only to discover that it is impossible to save myself with the self that gets me into trouble in the first place. I have judged others to be unable to handle the truth, unable to extend grace, unable to understand me, and I have ended up trapped in lies, law, and more loneliness. And I have judged God to be disappointed in me, distant from me, or unjust in his dealings with me, only to be overwhelmed by his love-without-reason again and again.

I have judged legalists and addicts, fundamentalists and universalists, Democrats and Republicans, faithful church attendees and those who worship in the mountains every weekend. I have made judgments about music, movies, sermons, alcohol, ice cream, football teams, parenting principles, churches, books, and restaurants. Obviously, to be human is to make judgments, but ever since the garden of Eden, what has gotten us into trouble is being certain that *our* judgments are the right ones, the ones that clearly sort out what is good and what is evil. I know that's what caused the estrangement in my relationship with my friends all those years ago. I thought that I was right, that I had been wronged, and that I certainly knew a lot more about grace than they did. Maybe they believed the same about themselves. All I know for sure is that there wasn't enough room in our friendship for all our judgments, so we parted company and lost contact with each other, until recently.

My friends' son told me about his decision to join the staff of a ministry that would give him opportunities to talk about Jesus on college campuses and around the world. He talked about a revitalized faith that had compelled him to forgo medical school for a while, because "life is short, and I want it to mean something eternal," he explained. He asked if I would consider supporting him. He asked if he could pray for me. And all those judgments no longer seemed important. I sensed God's redeeming path connecting us in and around the judgments we'd made along the way. I smiled at a God who could turn broken relationships into the gospel!

This event reminded me of another time when my judgments were transformed. Two years ago, I spent ten days in a solitary retreat in southwestern Colorado. During this retreat, I spent most of my time in reading and meditation, directed by a retreat leader. Once a day, we met for further direction and to provide an opportunity for me to ask questions and express frustration with all this quiet! The retreat leader spoke to me one morning about the importance of confession in making room in our souls for the unconditional love of Christ. I knew that I had things I needed to confess, and I strongly felt that I needed to confess them to a person. After knocking on a few church doors in town, I discovered that only one was open—a small Catholic church. Now, I'm not Catholic, and I've probably made a few ridiculous judgments about Catholics in my life, but I was growing desperate to speak to someone. A priest was at the front of this church, so I approached him and explained that I wasn't Catholic but that I wanted to make a confession. He guided me to the front pew, and we sat down side by side. Finally, I looked at him and began my litany of failures, mistakes, and sins. He listened patiently and then was quiet for quite a while after I finished. I was sure that I had overwhelmed him and that he was wondering where he might send me for further help, but just as I was getting ready to excuse myself, he placed his hand on my forehead and closed his eyes. When he opened his eyes, he peered into mine with an intensity that startled me, and then he said, "You have been judged, and you are forgiven." I walked out of that church with a lightness in my heart that I really can't describe. What a relief to know that I am completely known and completely forgiven!

Only God can turn judgment into good news. It's what I

call "redemptive judgment." Judgment that is for the purpose of redemption never gets stuck in the wrong that has been done but always turns to the greater right that was accomplished on the cross. My pastor says it this way: "There is only one judgment that can cut out the sin and save the sinner. The judgment is Love, come to us as Truth. God, come to us as Jesus. He is truth hanging on a cross, truth bleeding for us, truth broken for us. So we begin to believe truth because it's love, and we begin to believe love because it's true. It's Jesus, and we are to speak Jesus. *He's the judgment we are to give*."[8]

Our judgments can get in the way of our receiving the gift of estrangement. Our judgments also remind us that we need Someone outside of ourselves to give us perspective. We don't see ourselves clearly. Our judgments can keep us trapped in self-righteousness and indignation or in shame and self-contempt. Christ's death on the cross sets us free from all shame and condemnation, and it reminds us that there is only One who is completely righteous.

If you had the opportunity to confess all that is in your heart, what would you say? Write out your confession. Include a confession of your sins but also of your responses to the ways that others have hurt you. Read Romans chapter 8, which concludes with, "None of this fazes us because Jesus loves us. I'm absolutely convinced that nothing—nothing living or dead, angelic or demonic, today or tomorrow, high or low, thinkable or unthinkable—absolutely *nothing* can get between us and God's love because of the way that Jesus our Master has embraced us" (Rom. 8:37–39, italics added). If an estranged relationship is keeping you from experiencing God's love—either because you are too angry or too ashamed—can you exchange your judgments for God's judgments? Believe that you are forgiven, and ask God to heal whatever is keeping you from feeling his love. Holding on to anger and self-righteousness keeps us from experiencing the love of God, and that is perhaps the greatest sin of all. An estranged relationship and all of the pain and defensiveness it causes becomes the most powerful context for us to know we need grace and mercy, neither of which we can conjure up or bestow on ourselves.

The Redemption of Estrangement

After a year of virtually no contact, I got a call from Kristin. She needed help and support; she needed her mother. I was overwhelmingly grateful for the call, but I also felt a little guarded. I didn't want to get hurt again. I knew that I didn't trust myself not to withhold an open heart to her and that I didn't trust Kristin not to pull away again, but I did trust something in our hearts. I trusted my heart, full of love for my dear daughter, and I trusted her heart, full of love for me. Our love had been hijacked by a set of unfortunate but necessary circumstances. I wasn't sure what those circumstances brought for Kristin, but I knew that they had been a crucifixion for me. I knew I was ready to reconnect with my daughter, because of two disciplines a dear friend taught me / to practice in the midst of crucifixion: blessing the pain in the relationship and blessing the sweetness in the relationship.

Blessing the Pain in a Relationship

The best definition I've found for *blessing* is "to give thanks, to say that something is good." It's easy to see the heartache and misfortune in an estranged relationship, but it is essential to give thanks for the pain. When we don't bless the pain, the loss of what was or what might have been, we turn to the next moment with a rigidity that demands that it make up for how we have been hurt. We become women who require that others make up for all that we've lost in our estranged relationship. During my estrangement from my daughter, I didn't realize what I was doing to my son until he kindly pointed out, "Mom, do you realize you ask me if I've heard from Kristin before you ask anything about me?"

We can bless the pain if we have truly surrendered to suffering as the way of transformation. This blessing allows us to wait for the next moment with openness, knowing that even if we are hurt again, we can bear it because we know where — or to Whom — to turn. When we bless the pain, we acknowledge our suffering. It is there. We feel it. But it is necessary for our transformation. This keeps us from becoming rigid and demanding of others to heal our pain.

Giving thanks for our pain and calling it "good" does not come naturally. One morning, I awoke filled with sorrow and regret over my relationship with my daughter. I did not know how I could possibly find anything to bless in this estrangement. I began by telling God the truth and asking him for eyes to see, ears to hear, and a heart open to blessing. This is some of what I wrote in my journal that morning:

> God, thank you for the tears that will not stop. They remind me that I can feel.
>
> Thank you for the anguish I feel in missing my daughter. I have been blessed to have such a close relationship with her that this estrangement feels unbearable.
>
> Thank you for the guilt I feel over my failure. It guides me to you, the source of forgiveness.
>
> Thank you for Kristin's anger and hurt. She has been blessed with passion.
>
> Thank you for her opinions. You have given her a good mind.
>
> Thank you for the loneliness. It reminds me that I was made for relationships.

Thank you for the ache that remains. It reminds me that I was made for you.

Write your own prayer of gratitude for all the blessings that have come through the broken relationship in your life. Begin by listing all the difficulties you've experienced—guilt, anger, sorrow—and then give thanks for what those realities have created in you. For example, anger has compelled you to pause, look at the sorrow beneath the anger, and seek God's help in not expressing anger in destructive ways. If you can't find anything to be grateful for in a particular experience of this estranged relationship, confess that to God and ask him to show you the blessing in the midst of the difficult reality.

Blessing the Sweetness in a Relationship

Blessing the sweetness in a relationship prevents bitterness and resentment. When we experience an estrangement, often we choose to remember only the negative to minimize the enormity of our loss. We rewrite history by editing anything good. Unintentionally, we are also editing our future, because we will tend to view future relationships with cynicism or a jaded spirit, almost expecting to be hurt again, so we don't fully offer ourselves.

When I bless the sweet times in a relationship, I can let go and turn to give of that sweetness to others. I can recall good times together, and every time they come to mind, I can pray for the other person. Clearly, this is harder when the relationship is estranged. How do I bless the sweetness when the pain sometimes overwhelms me? My friend who taught me these disciplines, author and psychologist Dan Allender, wisely writes, "All harm is a gift that points us to the necessity of forgiveness and the promise of reconciliation. Harm reveals the finality of the cross and the utter open possibilities of the resurrection. Bless your enemies—they have delivered you to the cross more often and with greater necessity than your friends.... The brokenness of loss sings of potentiality of desire renewed."[9]

During my estrangement from Kristin, I kept a journal for her. I wrote the things I would want to tell her if we were talking. I told her about events in my life, and I remembered experiences that we had together. The journal allowed me to stay in touch with the sweetness of our relationship, and it also became a sweet gift to Kristin when we reconciled. We spent a few hours reading the journal and sharing with one another the moments we'd missed and remembering the moments that we'd shared.

Consider making a journal for the person you are estranged from. You can write your thoughts and prayers about the relationship, past, present, and future. You won't necessarily ever share this journal with the other person, but it can become a way for you to keep your heart open to both the joy and the sorrow in this relationship.

Months of blessing both the pain and the sweetness in my relationship with Kristin prepared me for her return to me and my return to her. I am actually grateful today for the estrangement because of the transformation this crucifix-

> *We dare not look at anyone, including the person staring back at us in the mirror, and conclude, 'Broken beyond repair.' Jesus still leaves the ninety-nine for the one little lamb who is in desperate need. Jesus is coming after you . . . and he is reaching through you to many others. He is ready to prove the wonders of his love and multiply more.*
>
> —Steven Curtis Chapman and Scotty Smith, *Restoring Broken Things*

ion worked in me. I am not naive enough to think I won't be tempted again by a need to be right, a need to make things work, and a need to be loved, but I no longer believe that the New Testament words about our carrying a cross are just an illustration. I know that being crucified is God's way of making me more like Jesus. I also know he will not leave us hanging on a cross. His is not only the way of the cross but also the way of the empty tomb. My relationship with my daughter is being restored, and in the midst of that restoration, I am reminded again and again that God makes all things new. And how does he accomplish this newness? Resurrection comes only when a crucifixion has first taken place. "What an *honor* to be crucified! Why? Because beyond crucifixion is resurrection."[10]

The desert of estrangement is lonely and makes us cry out, "If there is any other way, please take this pain from me." We echo the words of Jesus in the garden of Gesthemane as he faced crucifixion. Jesus' response models for us the way of transformation. He surrendered to the Father: "Your will be done" (Matt. 26:42 NIV). Surrender allows crucifixion. Resistance prolongs the pain and preempts any transformative work from occurring. We discover the meaning of estrangement when we encounter the cross and surrender to God's will, not our own. Look at your broken relationship through the eyes of God. Whether it be his only begotten Son or you, God favors crucifixion for one reason and one reason only: resurrection. The desert of estrangement has a wonderful purpose: it is where humility, mercy, trust, compassion, and forgiveness are resurrected!

Just for You

---

1. Recall experiences of relational failure from your past. How do you deal with the memories of this experience? Do you try not to think

about them? Do you obsess about them? Consider confessing those memories to God.

2. What would change in your life if you accepted the pain of an estranged relationship as a crucifixion from God?

3. Has an estranged relationship revealed attitudes and behaviors in you that might need to be destroyed? What are they?

4. How has your resistance to suffering impacted your spiritual life?

5. What is true of you today that would not be true without the painful relationships in your life?

6. In a painful relationship, what judgments did you make that you now need to let go of? For example, did you make a judgment that you deserve to be treated harshly or that you can never trust others because of this broken relationship?

7. What can you bless about the pain and the sweetness in this relationship? Consider writing a prayer of blessing about this relationship, including both the pain and the sweetness.

CHAPTER SIX

The Fruit of Loneliness

Pray that your loneliness may spur you into finding
something to live for, great enough to die for.

—Dag Hammarskjöld,
Markings

I HAVE FELT IT in a house full of people. I have felt it at the
end of a busy day, after I've done everything I'm supposed to
do. I have felt it while driving to the grocery store. It has sat
with me in church. It has joined me at the table with family
for Thanksgiving dinner. It has been waiting for me as I have
stepped off airplanes in some of the most interesting cities in
the world. It has wrapped itself around my heart and mind
after I have finished speaking, sharing intimate details about
my life. It has been present even on a great day, when something amazing happened. It has been my constant companion on a hard day, when I had to face painful realities. I have
willed it to go away, but it returns, proving it is stronger than

my will. I have tried to numb myself to it with food, alcohol, shopping, work, or people-pleasing, only to find that it is strengthened by these attempts to escape. I have prayed for it to go away, and it becomes part of my prayer.

Loneliness.

Whether you are in a life-giving relationship or suffering some of the difficult realities explored in previous chapters, you know loneliness. Loneliness can make us feel restless, irritable, discontent, sad, ashamed, angry, depressed, and even hopeless. We usually regard loneliness as an enemy. When it slithers through the cracks and makes us feel all these conflicting emotions, we know that it is a malevolent intruder. It makes us feel on edge, even desperate at times, desperate to find something or someone to keep us company.

Are you able to recognize and acknowledge loneliness in your life, or is it an emotion you try to suppress? It might be helpful to spend a week taking note of all of the times when you feel lonely. You might express your feelings out loud. When you're waiting in traffic, after you've had a frustrating conversation with your husband, upon leaving a wonderful dinner with friends, or when all the kids are tucked in bed, simply say, "I feel lonely." Then notice how you respond to your loneliness. Do you berate yourself for feeling it, dismiss it, diminish it, or simply grab a pint of ice cream and click on the television, hoping to lose your own reality in a little reality TV?

As I began to acknowledge and feel my loneliness, I found a shift of focus in these astounding words from Henri Nouwen: "What once seemed such a curse has become a blessing. All the agony that threatened to destroy my life now seems like the fertile ground for greater trust, stronger hope, and deeper love.... *Loneliness became the ground of my greatest fruitfulness.*"[1]

Fruitfulness? The only fruit produced from my loneliness was self-contempt, resentment, shame, and some patterns of addictive behavior. My attempts to control my loneliness left me feeling anything but fruitful, but I didn't know how else to respond. My experience echoed the sentiments of screen-writer and producer Joss Whedon, who wrote, "Loneliness is about the scariest thing out there."

But Nouwen's words seemed to suggest that loneliness has a divine purpose, and I was intrigued by that. Perhaps trying to control it, rather than learning to surrender to it, is what keeps us from understanding God's intention for loneliness. If so, then our task is to completely change our perception of loneliness so that God can reprogram our souls. Our response to loneliness determines whether we will live in the prison of control, as I had most of my life, or in the productivity of sur-render, as Nouwen's experience suggests.

The Prison of Control

Six months ago, I walked into a place I never intended to be. I handed over my driver's license, removed my jewelry, and left all my personal belongings behind. I received a clip-on badge with a number—no name—and that became my identity. I followed a woman through a metal detector, which immedi-ately beeped my infraction—I had forgotten to take off my watch. After surrendering my watch, I was led through a series of doors. One door slid open as another slid shut behind me. There were no windows. My guide turned to me and said, "I hope you aren't claustrophobic." After walking down a long hallway, the guide pushed a button on the wall, which released a drawer. She placed a metal identification chip into the drawer; it closed and then opened again, producing a key. "This will let us into the room," she said. We were surrounded by closed doors. The circulated air seemed to whisper, "You can't get out. You are locked in."

This was jail.

I had volunteered to participate in an Alcoholics Anonymous meeting in the Douglas County Correctional Center. I hadn't known what to expect, and I was immediately overwhelmed by the harsh realities of confinement. As nine women filed into our quickly relocked room, I noted the apparel of captivity. Everyone wore what looked like scrubs, only these clothes quickly identified the owners' residence: the Department of Corrections. Most women wore orange, which I learned represented that they were in minimum security. One woman wore navy blue. She was a trustee. She had been incarcerated for eleven months. They all wore flip-flops—no nail polish, jewelry, or makeup. As we began the meeting, I didn't know that these women, so obviously out of control of their own lives, were about to teach me something about surrender.

> *The dread of loneliness is greater than the fear of bondage.*
>
> —Germaine Greer,
> *The Madwoman's Underclothes*

We began our meeting and started to talk about the Twelve Steps, specifically Step 3: "We made a decision to turn our will and our lives over to the care of God." Several women spoke about their experiences with surrender. One woman who had just been sentenced to a year's imprisonment talked about her difficulty with this step: "I just can't surrender. I need to be in control." Considering that she was incarcerated, the irony of this woman's confession was clear, and it didn't take long for me to realize that I still hang on to my own ironic illusions of control.

Instead of surrendering my loneliness to God, I have surrendered it to denial, addiction, and contempt, only to end up in bondage to choices and behaviors that didn't alleviate the loneliness and certainly didn't give me freedom. While sitting in the suffocating confines of the Department of Corrections, it suddenly made much more sense to surrender my loneliness to the care of God. Sitting there, it was easy to see that he could do a much better job of caring for it than I could.

As I stepped out of the Douglas County jail—grateful to be holding my purse, looking at the mountains, and breathing fresh air—I renewed my desire to surrender my loneliness to Someone outside myself. Perhaps Nouwen was right, that surrendered loneliness can become the ground for fruitfulness. If that's true, then our capacity to surrender loneliness becomes our capacity to experience fruitfulness.

> *Their prison is only in their minds, yet they are in that prison, and so afraid of being taken in that they cannot be taken out.*
>
> —C. S. Lewis, *The Last Battle*

The Productivity of Surrender

In his book *Principle-Centered Leadership*, Stephen Covey explains the process for growing fruit, "According to natural laws and principles, I must prepare the ground, plant the seed, cultivate, and water if I expect to reap the harvest."[2] Covey explores the metaphor in the context of growing one's leadership skills, but the same principles apply to other kinds of personal and spiritual growth. If we want to pursue the spiritual fruitfulness Nouwen talks about, the question is, How do we prepare the ground, plant seeds, cultivate, and water loneliness? This is the question I began to think about in new ways last spring when I planted my first-ever vegetable garden. My father has farmed since he was a boy, and I have watched him plant a garden year after year, without a lot of interest on my part. As I began to look at the barren ground of my loneliness and consider Nouwen's observations about the fruitfulness of his loneliness, I developed an interest in gardening.

My dad came over last April to help me prepare the ground for my garden. He came again a few weeks later, and we planted the seeds. At that point, I thought we were done, and I could almost taste the fresh vegetables I anticipated I would harvest. My dad showed up a few weeks after planting and began to teach me about cultivating the garden. As the weeds grew faster than the vegetables, cultivating was not my favorite part of this experience. Since I live in Colorado, a relatively arid state, I also had to learn about watering my garden. I will share with you the results of my first-and-only attempt at gardening a little later, but it was during this process that I thought about loneliness in terms of preparing the ground, planting seeds, cultivating, and watering.

As my dad and I rototilled the ground, raked, and fertilized, I learned that preparing the ground requires letting go of a need for immediate results. Preparing the ground is hard work, with no fruit in sight. It is a time when you lay the groundwork and let go. When it was time to plant, my dad brought several packets of seeds. My excitement grew as I saw the pictures of bountiful harvest on the packages. I wanted to scatter the seeds across the prepared ground, water them, and find vegetables the next morning. I learned that planting seeds is a time to avoid scrambling, as my dad patiently showed me how to carefully move away a level of soil, carefully place a determined number of seeds, carefully cover the seeds—and wait. Preparing the ground took effort, planting the seeds required care, but cultivating the garden was the hardest part. Every morning I eagerly ran out to my little patch of growing vegetables only to find a patch overgrown with weeds. I quickly learned that cultivating a garden is not possible without persistence. I called my dad on a few occasions and complained, "The weeds are winning!" He patiently coached me, "Just wait." I would have stopped pulling those darn weeds if my dad hadn't given me hope. My dad also taught me a few tricks about irrigating, and I discovered that the result of preparing the ground faithfully, planting seeds carefully, and cultivating persistently was that I could get up early every morning and water my garden with a sweet contentment that came from trusting the process.

My little vegetable garden taught me to let go, take care, persist hopefully, and give in to contentment! I began to think further about these four practices and how they might allow loneliness to become good ground for fruitfulness.

Preparing the Ground by Letting Go

It is possible to experience loneliness with all of its sadness, disappointment, and hurt and not be consumed by it. When everything in me yearns for something to take away my loneliness, I prepare the ground for relational and spiritual fruit to grow out of the loneliness by letting go of my need to get rid of these uncomfortable emotions. I surrender to being comfortable with being uncomfortable. I have discovered that the easiest way for me to let go is to confess the truth of my feelings to Jesus, not so he can make me feel better or to take the emotions away but simply to ask him to be with me in the midst of them. Of course, he is always with me, but surrendering to his presence in the midst of uncomfortable emotions gives me a sense of his presence.

> *The seed cast in the gravel — this is the person who hears and instantly responds with enthusiasm. But there is no soil of character, and so when the emotions wear off and some difficulty arrives, there is nothing to show for it.*
>
> —Matthew 13:20–21

When my dad and I prepared the ground for my vegetable garden, we spent a lot of time softening the soil and then (with a handkerchief covering my nose and mouth), we worked a few wheelbarrows of manure into the soil. Preparing the ground is a metaphor for softening our hearts even, and maybe especially, in the unpleasant emotional realities in our lives. What happens to our hearts when we're upset, disappointed, stressed, or hurt? Surrendering to simply being with Jesus during these hard times softens our hearts. Sadly, in our confused, chaotic jumble of emotions and experiences, we often surrender to behaviors that harden our hearts and prevent us from growing any fruit. When you feel left out by your husband or friends, do you eat, get angry, or organize your closets? When you are stressed out, do you sleep, exercise, eat potato chips, or have a glass of wine? When you have a fight with your adolescent daughter, do you go shopping, clean the house, or call all your friends and tell them how awful she is? Preparing the ground so that fruit will grow requires that we allow uncomfortable emotions to soften our hearts and surrender to our need to just be with Jesus — confessing, praying, crying, talking — simply to be with him without any immediate results.

> *The seed cast in the weeds is the person who hears the kingdom news, but weeds of worry and illusions about getting more and wanting everything under the sun strangle what was heard, and nothing comes of it.*
>
> —Matthew 13:22

Planting Seeds as We Take Care

When my dad showed up with packets of seeds, my first impulse was to scatter those seeds as fast as I could in hopes that vegetables would pop up immediately. My dad taught me that planting effectively means taking care. Seeds can't take root when we scramble, frantically trying to avoid our loneliness or to come up with something to save us from it. When we don't take care of our hearts in the midst of loneliness, we are vulnerable to carelessly wandering all over the place, inappropriately seeking food, drink, activities, or people to comfort us. Taking the necessary care to plant seeds that will produce relational and spiritual fruit requires us to believe that loneliness is not a problem to be solved. We can settle down and have some compassion and respect for ourselves. A Japanese poet wrote, "If you want to find meaning, stop chasing so many things." We can paraphrase that for our purposes: "If you want to plant something, stop running away."

As we stay in the loneliness, turning to Jesus to be with us in this uncomfortable reality, we can care for ourselves in ways that make planting seeds possible. This self-care includes physical care: exercise, deep-breathing, and an occasional manicure and pedicure! Self-care includes emotional care: talking with friends, participating in a support group, journaling your thoughts and feelings. And self-care includes spiritual care: participating in a faith community, reading God's Word, meditating and worshiping. These aren't new ideas, but I am always intrigued by our resistance or reluctance to maintain a program of self-care. After asking this question for years and observing its reality in my life and the lives of other women, I have come to the conclusion that we don't maintain a life of self-care because we get frustrated that it doesn't make our loneliness go away. And then we start scrambling again, falsely hoping that there's something out there that can make the loneliness go away, rather than believing that loneliness is a cue to take care of ourselves so that during our loneliness we can plant seeds that will grow beautiful fruit.

When my dad helped me plant my garden, he picked the seeds that he thought would grow best in our Colorado soil. We planted beans, zucchini, tomatoes, and spinach, and I expected that beans, zucchini, tomatoes, and spinach would grow. What seeds can we plant in our loneliness? If we want to grow "the fruit of the Spirit ... love, joy, peace, patience, kindness, goodness, faithfulness, gentleness and self-control" (Gal. 5:22–23 NIV), then we need to plant those seeds. Planting joy when we feel the sadness of loneliness seems counterintuitive, unless we are taking care of ourselves during the planting process. When I'm caring for myself—body, soul, and spirit— I can plant a little joy even in the midst of sadness, because I have nourished my heart rather than starving it.

I have a friend who has modeled caring for oneself and planting seeds in loneliness. She lost her mother this past year and has grieved deeply the loss of this close relationship. She takes care of herself by walking with three friends every morning, and she participates in a grief group at her church. Out of her self-care, she has been able to plant seeds in the lives of others. Once a week she sends a note to a young mother in her church. In the note, she reflects on her relationship with her own mother, comments on qualities she has noticed in the young mother's parenting, and includes a special treat for the mom like a gift certificate to Starbucks or a coupon for an hour or two of free babysitting. My friend is hurting, but she is caring for herself in the midst of her pain. My friend is so lonely for her mother, but she is planting seeds in her loneliness that I know will grow beautiful fruit in her life and in the lives of many moms.

Cultivating Fruit as We Persist in Hope

Cultivating anything—whether it's a vegetable garden or a life characterized by faith, love, and joy—is a slow process; it requires persistence. *Cultivating* means "to tend or nurture what has been planted." During my garden experiment, I learned that cultivating meant continuing to keep the ground prepared while tending to any weeds that might choke out my vegetables, and getting up and doing it all over, again and again. Cultivating relational and spiritual fruit out of loneliness is possible only if I have prepared my heart by remaining soft and vulnerable during difficult and disappointing experiences, by taking care of myself in the midst of the loneliness, and by remaining committed to this process day in and day out. Every morning when I ran out to the backyard to check on my vegetable garden, I had to face the weeds that had grown overnight. Loneliness that pops up even when we are taking care of ourselves and planting good seeds can feel as disheartening as the sight of all those thorns and thistles. When I feel discouraged or lose faith that all those seeds will really produce any kind of fruit, I think of some brave people I know who are persisting in hope in the midst of their loneliness:

> *When anyone hears news of the kingdom and doesn't take it in, it just remains on the surface, and so the Evil One comes along and plucks it right out of that person's heart.*
>
> —Matthew 13:19

- The woman whose daughter told her to "get the hell out of her life."
- The daughter who really does want "the hell" out of her life.
- The mom whose son is in Iraq and has not heard from him in three weeks.
- The young woman struggling with infertility who has a hard time celebrating the birth of a friend's baby.

- The middle-aged mom with the sweet, sweet baby girl who sometimes has over a hundred seizures an hour.
- The exhausted mother who placed her teenage son in a six-month treatment facility and is wondering what she did wrong and whether what she is doing now is right.
- The many, many single women who are trying to decide which feels less lonely during the holidays—trying to fit in with someone else's family celebration or going to a movie by themselves on Christmas.

These stories remind me that preparing our hearts, taking care of ourselves, and planting seeds of the fruit of the Spirit (patience, kindness, self-control, and so on; see Gal. 5:22–23) does not mean that my loneliness will go away. Persisting in the process of growth—keeping my heart soft, taking care of myself, planting good seeds—requires hope. Our hope is not that the loneliness will go away but that as we remain committed to the process of growth, the loneliness will become more bearable and continue to be the context in which we prepare the ground, plant seeds, and cultivate fruit.

When people get lost in the circumstances of their loneliness, they lose faith—faith in God, in others, and in themselves. When I was experiencing a season of intense loneliness, my pastor reminded me, "Despair isn't the natural state of things. God is. And he is hope. So we don't achieve hope; we die, feeling like we're drowning in hopelessness, to then take a breath and realize that for the first time, we're breathing and home." I love those words, because they remind me of how growth occurs. We seldom see it. We don't go to bed at night proclaiming, "I grew today." Growth happens as we hang in there and cultivate the practices of health and wholeness. Growth is going on even when we feel despair and confusion about our circumstances. Growth takes place while we are letting go. It may even feel like we are losing our life. We surrender, take a deep breath, and surrender again. And then one day we don't hate the loneliness; our hearts remain soft when we are hurt or misunderstood, self-care is the natural rhythm of our lives, and we catch our reflection in the midst of another lonely experience and are able to say, "I've grown."

When you feel like you are drowning in loneliness, hang on. Persist. A great harvest is coming. The loneliness of your life is the perfect place for fruit to grow. But you have to surrender to waiting, knowing that as you persist, God is doing work deep down where no one can see, hoping with you for beautiful fruit.

Now would be a good time to note what you do when nagging loneliness makes you discouraged. Do you harden your heart by telling yourself that you were stupid for hoping for anything? Do you abandon self-care because you give up? Discouragement is a cue that we need to persist, to continue in life-giving practices even when there is no evidence of fruit. During my gardening experiment last summer, I got discouraged and complained to my dad, "I don't think anything is growing in that dirt!" He asked me, "Sharon, will you commit to water and weed every day for the next three weeks?" He knew me well enough to know that when I don't see results, I often abandon the task. I made the commitment to water and weed, which allowed me to focus less on growing the fruit and more on my responsibility. My dad reminded me, "God's the only one who can grow the fruit. You're the only one who can water and weed."

Can you commit to cultivating fruit in the midst of your loneliness, even if you don't see any fruit? Perhaps you can commit to a program of self-care or to planting seeds of kindness. Call a friend and share your commitment. We are more likely to persist in our responsibilities when we have the support of others.

Growing Fruit as We Give in to Contentment

We tend to believe that contentment comes when we arrive at a place where things are working. We have what we want, our relationships are flourishing, and we are who we hoped we would be. But contentment is more about giving in than it is about arriving. Consider the words the apostle Paul wrote from jail: "Actually, I don't have a sense of needing anything personally. I've learned by now to be quite content whatever my circumstances. I'm just as happy with little as with much, with much as with little. I've found the recipe for being happy whether full or hungry, hands full or hands empty. Whatever I have, wherever I am, I can make it through anything in the One who makes me who I am" (Phil. 4:11 – 13).

> *The seed cast on good earth is the person who hears and takes in the News, and then produces a harvest beyond his wildest dreams.*
>
> —Matthew 13:23

When we give up the delusion that "When I acquire, marry, become ..., I will be happy" and give in to being content with whatever we have and wherever we are, we can water and grow real relational and spiritual fruit.

I need to give in to contentment a hundred times a day. I need to drop the ideal of who I think I ought to be, who I think I want to be, and who I think other people think I want or ought to be. When I give in to contentment, I believe that loneliness is not a threat. It is not punishment. Giving in is a grace-laden decision that declares that nothing—not relationships, not achievement, not success, not failure—has value without trust in the merciful love of God. Giving in is how we say, "Yes, I trust God." The psalmist said it this way, "Blessed are you who give yourselves over to GOD, turn your backs on the world's 'sure thing,' [and] ignore what the world worships" (Ps. 40:4).

I loved my early morning watering time in the garden last summer. It was a time of rest because I knew that I had prepared the ground, planted good seeds, and cultivated the garden with continued care. My morning time in the garden was a time of rest because I knew that growing the fruit was up to God. Oh, there were times when I wished that I could will those vegetables to grow, but I knew there was nothing further I could do but give in to contentment. The garden was in God's hands.

Contentment allows us to move from anxiety about our loneliness, to faith that our loneliness can be the ground of great fruitfulness, and then to release when we accept that growing the fruit is up to God. We give in to contentment when we know that we have done our part and we trust God with his responsibility. Are you waiting for fruit to grow in some of your relationships? Are you waiting for fruit to grow in your own life as you faithfully prepare, plant, and water seeds of self-care and spiritual discipline? Can you move from anxiety to faith to release? Note what you are anxious about. What is keeping you from believing that the difficulty, the waiting, or the loneliness is a good place for fruit to grow? The answer to that question may reveal where you need to soften your heart further by surrendering to just being with Jesus, to practice self-care, or to plant a few more seeds without needing to see the fruit. Can you release the rest to God, trusting that it's his job, and his alone, to grow the fruit?

The Fruit of Loneliness

One summer a friend of mine decided that every time she felt lonely, she would plant a different flower in her backyard garden. She called it her "freedom garden"—freedom from trying to control her own life, freedom in surrendering to God, freedom in trusting that loneliness would become the ground for fruitfulness. That summer she planted hundreds of flowers, and by the end of the summer, she had a garden that the neighbors not only took time to enjoy but brought friends along to view the spectacular array of flowers. My friend surveyed her garden at the end of the summer and said, "I must have been pretty lonely this summer." I replied, "Well, you can look at it that way or you can say, 'I've been pretty fruitful this summer!'" The New Testament also describes a freedom garden: "But what happens when we live God's way? ... fruit appears ... things like affection for others, exuberance about life, serenity. We develop a willingness to stick with things, a sense of compassion in the heart, and a conviction that a basic holiness permeates things and people. We find ourselves involved in loyal commitments, not needing to force our way in life, able to marshal and direct our energies wisely" (Gal. 5:22–23).

> *Study this story of the farmer planting seed. . . . Ripe, holy lives will mature and adorn the kingdom of their Father.*
>
> —Matthew 13:18, 43

My friend's freedom garden is a wonderful tangible representation of loneliness producing fruit in her life. As for my vegetable garden last summer? I'm sad to say the only thing I successfully grew was zuchinni, and I had enough for myself, my family, my friends, and my neighborhood! My dad encouraged me, "Gardening is not for the faint of heart." I'm not sure gardening is for me at all, but even though I will be buying my produce at Whole Foods from now on, I am grateful for the lessons I learned in the garden.

And I have also seen fruit grow in loneliness in ways that aren't so tangible. I want to share with you some fruit that I have seen so that it might give you ideas of what to look for in your own life as you prepare the ground by letting go, plant seeds by taking care, and cultivate fruit by hopefully persisting, and grow fruit as you give in to contentment.

Love

"Affection for others" and "a sense of compassion in the heart" (Gal. 5:22) grow when we stop asking, "Why does God allow me to be lonely?" and begin to ask, "Why don't I love more in the midst of all this loneliness?" My friends William and Dana are great examples of what it means to love more. William and Dana attend my church, and we are in the same small group. In this past year, William's sister, an alcoholic, committed suicide. William's mother died from a broken heart after the loss of her daughter. And both William and Dana lost their jobs and faced significant health problems. They know that many parts of the journey of grief must be walked alone, yet because of their sorrow, they are more in tune to the suffering of others. Their grief has not imprisoned them. In fact, whenever someone in our community is in an intense struggle, William and Dana are the first to be called. Their affection and compassion for others is fruit that has grown up between the painful, prickly thistles of lonely heartache, and I am so grateful that they are not keeping that fruit to themselves.

> *If we are hostage to ourselves, we will be imprisoned by loneliness.*
>
> —Henri Nouwen, *Intimacy*

Peace

Serenity in loneliness is fruit I often see in Twelve Step meetings. My friend Sally has shown me the fruit of peace, which also produces "a conviction that a basic holiness [can] permeate" any situation. Months ago, Sally's purse was stolen while she was in the grocery store. The thief used Sally's credit cards to charge over $20,000 in goods and services. Investigators were able to track down the woman who had stolen Sally's purse, and charges were filed. Sally attended the sentencing and asked the district attorney if she could speak before the judge sentenced her perpetrator. The district attorney recognized Sally. You see, Sally had charges pending in court as well. A few months before her purse was stolen, Sally had been arrested for driving under the influence. Sally's arrest began a journey of facing her alcoholism, realizing the significant role that loneliness played in her addictive behaviors, seeking help, confessing her foolishness and failure, and surrendering control to God. Even though she knew she might be sentenced to jail for her violation of the law, Sally grew a lot of peace during those first months of surrender.

The district attorney reminded Sally that her charges might be made known to the court if she testified in the case of her stolen purse. Sally calmly informed the DA, "Oh, I plan to tell the judge about my situation myself." When it was Sally's turn to make a statement about sentencing for the convicted thief, she turned and faced the terrified woman and said, "I will be standing in your shoes in a few weeks. I am guilty of a crime as well. At first, I wanted them to throw the book at you, but as I prayed about it, I knew what I really wanted was for you to experience the forgiveness and grace of God that I have come to know since I was charged with a DUI." Sally then handed the woman a Bible and sat down. The woman was sentenced to a fine and eight months in jail.

At the end of the summer, Sally was sentenced to six months in jail. There's one more way that I have experienced the fruit that has grown in Sally's life during her lonely walk of the past months. She is the one who invited me to the Alcoholics Anonymous meeting in the jail. She knows that she will spend a little time there soon, but I know that whether she is in or out of jail, the fruit of peace is evident in her life and available to others wherever she is and whatever circumstances she is in.

Passion

One who has cultivated the fruit of passion in the midst of loneliness has an "exuberance about life … a willingness to stick with things … [is] involved in loyal commitments … [and is] able to marshal and direct [energy] wisely" (Gal. 5:22–23). A wonderful fruit of surrendering our loneliness to God is that we become available for people, places, and things that we never would have been available for otherwise. When we no longer try to hide, numb, or deny our loneliness, passion has room to grow. Passion is often equated with romance or adventure, and certainly passion shows up in those experiences. But passion is more about being fully present to whatever or whoever is in front of you. Passion asks the question, "Why me, in this place, with these people, at this time?" Passion allows me to believe that I have something to offer in this moment, that others—no matter how different they may be from me—have something to offer me in this moment, and that God has orchestrated our being in this moment because he wants us to know something about him. When I don't believe that loneliness is a context for fruitfulness, I am tempted to believe that I don't have anything to offer because I conclude that loneliness makes me inferior. I believe that others don't have anything to offer me because loneliness has made me suspicious of others. And I don't look for God to grow unexpected fruit in unlikely places because I see loneliness as a punishment instead of a gift.

When I trust that loneliness is good ground for growing fruit, and I prepare my heart, care for myself, plant seeds, persist in cultivating, and trust God to grow the fruit, passion will grow—often in surprising places. Certainly one of those places for me is a tattoo parlor. I have two tattoos. One is a small heart on my right wrist. I got this tattoo for Christmas a few years ago after my then seventeen-year-old son taunted me, "Mom, you'd never get a tattoo." Well, I showed him and got my *Braveheart* tattoo and certainly lessened the desire for my teenage son to get something that his middle-aged mother got first! My other tattoo is on my left wrist. It is a white cross. If you look closely, in the right light, you can see it. It really looks more like a scar, which was my intention—to remind me that by Christ's scars we are healed, that wounds are where Love gets in.

I have taken a few people to this tattoo parlor, partly because it is inviting and clean but mostly because of a tattoo artist named Matt. Matt has "sleeves" of tattoos on his arms. On one of his hands, he has a tattoo with the words "tattooing for Jesus." When you ask him, "What's that about?" he simply replies, "That's why I'm doing what I do. It's for Jesus." He's passionate about his art, about people, and about his faith.

I recently took a former client, Emily, to get a tattoo in this tattoo parlor. She wanted a white cross on her ankle to represent her commitment to her faith. This was significant for Emily. When I met her four years ago, she was considering the Wiccan faith. After many conversations and Emily's own diligent search through the Scriptures, she committed her life to Christ. She explained, "The cross symbolizes my surrender."

Emily's tattoo was quite a bit different from my two tiny designs. Emily wanted her tattoo to be significant—something that would be hard to miss. I watched (for a few minutes at a time) as Emily got her tattoo. Matt worked for about three hours to permanently mark Emily with the cross. It hurts to get a tattoo of this magnitude. It bleeds. Matt explained, "If it didn't hurt, everyone would be covered with tattoos [I kind of doubt this], and you have to earn a tattoo." Emily winced, covered her face with her hands, and stiffened her body so that Matt could tenderly bring forth the image that Emily wanted to carry on her body for the rest of her life. As I watched Emily and Matt, I rejoiced that my loneliness has made room to know so many different people and to learn about passion from them.

The Most Beautiful Fruit

Emily and her cross tattoo and Matt the talented tattoo artist made me think. I have read that most people who get tattoos not only want to mark themselves with a particular message; they also want to proclaim that message to others. My tiny tattoos are really more reminders to myself than proclamations to others. I wondered what image I might have seared into my flesh if I wanted it to be the message that I would leave with others, a symbol of the fruit grown in my life because of my relationship with Jesus. I know the message that is most meaningful to me has to do with love, grace, mercy, and forgiveness. I have seen people who have these words tattooed on their skin in English or other languages, but to me that falls short of conveying the depth of meaning that these realities have for me. And I know that I don't have the courage or fortitude to get a tattoo that could fully tell the story of that message.

I once read in *Rolling Stone* magazine that tattoos are the "art of the soul of this generation." But engraving the flesh with a message is not new. The New Testament describes the art of the Soul of God when the doubting disciple Thomas met Jesus after the crucifixion. Jesus helped the doubter believe by marking his own body with his message: "Take your finger and examine my hands. Take your hand and stick it in my side. Don't be unbelieving. Believe" (John 20:27). Brennan Manning describes these marks (the holes in Jesus' hands, side, and feet) as "brilliant wounds of a battle long ago, almost like a signature carved in the flesh."[3] The signature of Jesus announces passionately, better than any words, "I would rather die than live one day without you." The most beautiful fruit of his loneliness for us was prepared in the heart of the Father, cultivated at Calvary, planted in a tomb, and brought to life in the resurrection—all for a chance to get close to us.

The brilliant wounds of Jesus reveal the Soul of God, but they are also intended to bring forth fruit in our lives. Seeing the signature of Jesus, really seeing it, allows no one to remain unchanged. I used to believe that we were all desperately searching for God in the midst of our loneliness, that our loneliness compels our search for something to fill the "God-shaped" hole inside of us. Experiencing redemption in the many lonely places of my story has taught me that the deepest story is that God is searching for us, and the wounds of Jesus are intended to invite me to surrender to the One who is surrendered to me.

The signature of surrender. Jesus has engraved it into his own body so that it might become the art of my soul in a passionate message that emanates from my story. Not that I crave something from God; I crave God. And God doesn't want something from me; he wants me. Perhaps that is the most beautiful fruit of loneliness—that in my loneliness I surrender to a lonely God, the Beautiful One who is surrendered to me. Without loneliness, I might miss him. God's presence abides in the midst of the ruins of loneliness, and it is in the midst of those same ruins that the most beautiful fruit is grown.

Just for You

1. Consider the role loneliness has played in your life. It may help to imagine that you are interviewing yourself at different ages: elementary school, high school, college, and so on. How would you describe your loneliness?

2. Complete this sentence: "When I am lonely, I ..."

3. How might your experience of loneliness change if you really believed that it has divine purposes?

4. As you consider surrendering your loneliness to the care of God, it would be good to be confident that he cares. Keep a daily journal. Take note of the ways that God cares for you each day. Write about it, take pictures that represent his care, or paste other artifacts into your journal that remind you of a specific way God cared for you. This practice will be most beneficial as you observe God's care of you over time, but you can profit from it more immediately as well. Look for God's care over the next week. Ask a friend to do the same, and then get together and share what you have observed about God's care in only one week.

5. Recall an experience of loneliness from your past. Looking back, do you now see any new life that grew out of that difficult season?

6. Read Galatians 5:22–23. Take note of the fruit listed. What fruit is in your life right now?

7. How might you love more in the midst of your loneliness? Make a list of people you might love and how you could love them.

Begin Again, Believe Again
in Redeeming Relationships

I know that my Redeemer lives, and that in the end he will stand upon the earth. And after my skin has been destroyed, yet in my flesh I will see God.

—Job 19:25–26 NIV

"Who are you?"

"I am the one loved by Christ."

—Thomas Merton

In part 3, the braverheart surrenders to trust again, hope again, and fall in love again because she knows, heart and soul, that daily and difficult human relationships contain the most intimate spiritual truths of all. The ache of longing represents the image of the One who longs for a relationship with us more than anything else. The pain of brokenness leads us to the Healer and the gifts that come in surrendering to his healing touch. The shame of personal failure opens the door to experience, to *feel*, the presence of the Savior. Loneliness reminds us of the lonely God who wanders through the garden, looking for us, asking, "Where are you?" Women willing to look like fools reveal the heart of the One who "though he was rich, yet for your sakes he became poor, so that you through his poverty might become rich" (2 Cor. 8:9 NIV). And the experiences in relationships when we absolutely do not know what to do, cannot bear to hear another well-meaning word of advice, and feel utter despair at understanding any of it, can give us ears to hear the whisperings of the only One who sees us, hears us, and understands us.

In chapter 7, we will look at trusting again, which seems questionable unless our faith is rooted in Someone who is more certain than all that we can see. As we learn to "hope for and [be] certain of what we do not see" (Heb. 11:1 NIV), relationships become the catalysts for making us women of great faith. Chapter 8 explores hoping again, which may seem foolish unless we believe that all the difficulties and disappointments in relationships are a way of bringing us home—really home—to our Father. When we learn to rest in relational struggles, the beautiful ache that remains for more in relationships becomes a gentle reminder that we are not home yet. In chapter 9, we will consider falling in love again, which may seem impossible unless our eyes are fixed stead-fastly on the One who loves us unreservedly. When we make human relationships about only those relationships, we write a smaller story for ourselves than God intended. When we allow human relationships, in all of their agony and glory, to transform us into women of faith, hope, and love, then we are living a deeper story. The braverheart believes again and again that her desire for relationships inevitably leads to the glory of transformation. "And we, who with unveiled faces [showing every bruise, mark, and scar] all reflect the Lord's glory, are being transformed into his likeness [also bruised, marked, and scarred], with ever-increasing glory" (2 Cor. 3:18 NIV).

CHAPTER SEVEN

Daring to Trust Again

When our trust has been betrayed and those who were supposed to stand by us don't, this naturally has consequences for how we think about God. It becomes hard to trust that God is good when our significant relationships simply aren't that good.

—Rob Bell, *Sex God*

"SHARON, LOOK AT ME. Look at me. I want to tell you in front of all these people that I will never be unfaithful to you. I will never leave you. I will never divorce you." I was only half listening to this declaration of undying love as I sat at the back of a hotel conference room filled with over five hundred people. It was September 9, 2000, and my husband of almost nineteen years was pledging his fidelity to me during a Family-Life marriage conference. We had been speakers for this ministry for about three years, and I had heard this promise many times. My husband almost always ended the conference by making this pledge to me. I was half listening because I took these words for granted, and they didn't mean that much to me. Although we were both speakers for a marriage ministry, our marriage really wasn't a priority, and we were living parallel but separate lives, which put our marriage in peril.

One year after that September marriage conference, my husband announced that he was lonely and that he didn't want to be married to me anymore. He packed two suitcases and moved into an extended-stay hotel a few miles from our home. I was shocked, humiliated, and devastated. And I believed that I would never trust anyone again.

Betrayal does that. Whether it is betrayal by a spouse, a child, a friend, our health, our job, our church, or ourselves, it leaves us feeling alone and paralyzed with grief. The events that unfolded in the ending of my marriage plunged me into a dark sea that I thought I could not and would not survive. I couldn't think clearly. I relapsed in my alcoholism. I watched my children drowning in their own woundedness and confusion, yet I felt incapable of helping them find safety. I retreated into isolation because I felt that my friends had grown tired of hearing about my troubles, and I believed that they didn't understand anyway. I got angry. I burned every family picture that included my husband. I was overwhelmed. I didn't open bills for months at a time. I was exhausted. There were many days in the first two years after our marriage exploded that I went to bed, pulled the blanket over my head, and prayed that I wouldn't wake up in the morning.

The evidence of a betrayal is often obvious—a divorce, estrangement, attendance at family functions and social events by yourself, photo albums filled with pictures of people who are no longer in your life. But the ruins of betrayal are not only external. Because we are designed for intimate, mutual relationships, we experience betrayal at a core level. Betrayal has a traumatic component that remains long after the actual experience. I have a friend who has had a difficult, lonely marriage. Her husband forgets her birthday every year. During the first years of marriage, she would drop hints and hope that he would remember the date. After a few years, my friend not only stopped hoping that her husband would celebrate her birthday; she refused to let anyone else celebrate it either. She explained, "It's just too hard to want something on that day. I'd rather pretend that it is an ordinary date."

When our design for intimate, mutual relationships is diminished or thwarted by the daily, difficult relationships that we all encounter, we feel betrayed. We might not identify it as a betrayal, but we experience it as one, and it shows up in our internal world when we trust a little less, our hearts become a little tougher, and we determine not to want so much.

Relationships that don't work shatter trust, but when we are determined not to try again, believe again, hope again, and risk again, we shatter ourselves even more. American journalist Norman Cousins studied the human condition, and after years of observing people, he concluded, "Death is not the great loss in life. The greatest loss is what dies inside us while we live."[1] When we are betrayed, the greatest loss may not be the loss of the relationship but the loss of our desire to want anything in relationships again. When painful relationships obliterate our capacity to trust, we can lose ourselves in emotional darkness, numbness, or self-hatred. And sooner or later, most of us also feel utterly abandoned by God. In the midst of our disillusionment with human relationships, we must also come to grips with a divine relationship—one that fails to rescue us from dark, painful places.

After I stopped burning pictures, rehearsing my husband's crimes, and scrambling to protect my self-image, I came face-to-face with God. I railed at him, "Where have you been?" "How could you allow this to happen?" and "How can I ever trust you again?"

The only thing I heard in response was deafening silence. I felt paralyzed with pain and trapped in a pit from which there was no escape. At its deepest level, my experience of betrayal stopped me from going through the motions as if nothing significant had happened, and it began to alter my basic makeup. I could no longer make things work, and I couldn't pretend that everything was okay. Although I couldn't see it at the time, I realize now that I was in a state of grace, that I had found *favor* with God.

Pain is a place of potential grace, a showering of God's favor on us, because God longs to restructure our hearts and transform us from self-reliant people to God-reliant people. When betrayal shatters our lives and destroys our trust, we have a choice. We can collapse in bitterness, isolation, and the most destructive self-reliance of all: never wanting anything from anyone again. Or we can choose to believe that all relational pain is a means to convert us to a radical reliance on God, enabling us to live a "wide-open, spacious life" (2 Cor. 6:11).

Author Brennan Manning writes, "The grace-laden act of trust is the landmark decision of life outside of which nothing has value and inside of which every relationship and achievement, every success and failure derives it final meaning."[2] Manning goes on to explain that this surrender is "our decisive YES to Christ's command, 'Trust in God and trust in me.'"[3] The grace-laden act of trust and the decisive act of saying yes to God grows in us when, in the silence of God, we come to believe in the care of God; in the paralysis of pain, we learn to look for the protection of God; and in the pit of despair, we experience the rescue of God.

The Silence of God, the Care of God

The hard work of daily relationships and the pain of difficult relationships are often intensified because we feel the absence of God's presence. We can't hear him. We are wired for relationships and tend to evaluate our lives by our relationships, so the pain and confusion we experience in human relationships make our relationship with God suspect. If God loves us, what are we doing crawling over glass in human relationships? If we are daughters of the King of Heaven, why do we experience betrayal, injustice, and overwhelming difficulties? Why does God remain silent?

When we experience the silence of God, we can cave in to desolation—anger and despair—or we can seek consolation. It is part of the human experience to question God's presence, especially during painful times. Questioning God is actually an act of faith because it assumes his existence. It is human to experience anger and despair in our confusion about God and what he is up to. Staying stuck in desolation, however, is a protection against vulnerability and need. Moving out of our inevitable questions about God and toward consolation requires that we open our hearts and our hands and wait. This experience is when a person knows that things are not as they should be and will not rest until she hears from God. Only a person who ardently believes in God will have the courage to endure desolation and wait for consolation.

Desolation

Often when I experience a wound in relationships, I respond with my arms crossed, body tensed, and heart hardened, "Fine. I don't need anyone." That's a step toward desolation. *Desolation* is defined as "abandoned or forsaken; loneliness; wretchedness; misery; devastation; and ruin." When we feel emotionally abandoned, we want to hide. We hide when we numb our-selves with addictions such as food, alcohol, shopping, work-ing, or people-pleasing. We hide when we refuse to be open to God or to others. We hide when we harden our hearts, deter-mined to not feel anything, want anything, confess anything, risk anything, or hope for anything again. Hiding turns us in on ourselves. When we isolate ourselves in the midst of our pain and confusion, it's like walking alone through a danger-ous neighborhood; we place ourselves in harm's way. Hiding drives us down a dark spiral that takes us even deeper into our own negative feelings. It distorts our perspective by deluding us into thinking that it is God and not ourselves who has gone into hiding. The desola-tion that shrouds us when we hide compels us to give up on things that used to be impor-tant to us. It takes over our consciousness and crowds out our vision for the future. We retreat and then wonder why we receive no consolation from God and are confused by his apparent absence and silence.

> *Love makes your soul crawl out from its hiding place.*
>
> —Zora Neal Hurston,
> *I Love Myself When I Am Laughing ... and Then Again*

Consolation

To receive consolation is to be soothed, relieved, and calmed. All of these descriptors imply the experience of being distressed and waiting for comfort. I have a friend who says desolation is what she feels when God shuts the door to some-thing that she longs for, and consolation comes when God opens another door. But, she explains, waiting in the hallway can feel like hell.

David the psalmist knew about betrayal and desolation. After being made captain of all of Israel's armies and experiencing the praise of everyone, he was rejected and exiled by his mentor, King Saul, who wanted to kill him. He wrote about his experience of desolation.

> The hangman's noose was tight at my throat;
> devil waters rushed over me.
> Hell's ropes cinched me tight;
> death traps barred every exit.
> A hostile world!
>
> —Psalm 18:4–6

But David also knew what it meant to move from desolation to consolation.

> I call to GOD,
> I cry to God to help me.
> From his palace he hears my call;
> my cry brings me right into his presence—
> a private audience!
>
> —Psalm 18:6

David expressed the agony of abandonment and betrayal. He cried out to God. And then he waited. Waiting to hear from God requires trust; it requires that we keep our hearts open while we wait for whatever might be around the corner. We will not experience consolation unless we wait for it, which may seem counterintuitive when we have been hurt. It's natural to close our hearts to any further harm.

We learn to trust again—even when we are in the midst of desolation—when we simply come to God with the unvarnished truth about our lives. Hiding nothing, we come to him with our outrage, bewilderment, fear, hurt, and utter lostness. For two years after my world fell apart, I got up every morning and walked about two miles around my neighborhood. Sometimes I listened to music. Other times I talked to myself, rehearsing wrongs, previous conversations, and the things that I would say if I ever got a chance. Many mornings I cried and didn't think or say anything. I began to see those early morning walks as my way of simply coming to God.

During those dark days, a friend of mine told me about the meditation of a missionary named Brother Andrew: "He sees, he hears, he understands." On many mornings I repeated those words as I walked. I didn't completely believe them, but I didn't know what else I could trust. I came to God wanting to believe that he saw my situation, that he heard all the realities of my life and heart, and that he understood what I needed. I came to God wanting to believe, and in the process, *I came to believe.*

My experience of God's absence and my desperate, daily coming to him, simply repeating the words of Brother Andrew, created a space for God's presence—for a growing, more intimate relationship with him—and in time, I began to experience the consolation of God. Although my circumstances did not change, I felt less alone. As I meditated on God's care, I felt seen, heard, and understood by him. The New Testament promises, "He comes alongside us when we go through hard times" (2 Cor. 1:4).

We come to believe in the care of God when we come to him day in and day out, not hiding anything, and we wait for him to show up. When we stop hiding our hearts from God, our hearts soften and we move from desolation to wanting consolation. We must doggedly show up even when he seems not to. If that is not the warm and fuzzy practice you were hoping for, let me echo the disciples' question when their faith was shaken and they could not figure out what Jesus was up to: "Lord, to whom shall we go? You have the words of eternal life" (John 6:68 NIV).

The way of consolation—coming to trust in God's care—is not necessarily the way of happiness, but it is the way of rest. There is something very freeing about acknowledging not only our pain but our need for God to soothe our sorrows.

While I wait for God to minister to me, I may still feel hurt or confused, but there is peace in knowing that I cannot talk, think, or work myself out of this. Only a person who waits and whose soul cries out day and night to the living God will eventually experience the deep rest of consolation.

The way of consolation begins with telling the truth about how we've been hurt and our response of anger or confusion. Waiting for consolation then allows us to redirect our focus outside ourselves, knowing that we need a sense of God's presence to bring soothing and relief to our desolation. This daily practice of telling God the truth about our inner world and asking him for comfort restores balance; we are no longer focused only on the pain. We are waiting for God to be in the pain with us, speak words of solace to us, and give us hope that the pain is not all there is.

While we are traveling the way of consolation, our focus can also be directed to others who are experiencing desolation. Waiting for consolation should not be an experience of isolation. Even if we have not been completely comforted in our own wounds of disappointment or betrayal, offering comfort to others keeps us on the way of consolation. The New Testament describes the circle of consolation, "the Father of compassion and the God of all comfort, who comforts us in all our troubles, so that we can comfort those in any trouble with the comfort we ourselves have received from God" (2 Cor. 1:3–4 NIV). Staying on the way of consolation will show us where we need God, allow us to experience moments of comfort and calm, and compel us to offer comfort to others whom we meet along the way.

The psalmist illustrates the way of consolation. He describes what he experienced after he cried to God out of his desolation and waited for consolation. He encourages us with the comfort he found.

But me he caught—reached all the way
from sky to sea; he pulled me out
of that ocean of hate, that enemy chaos,
the void in which I was drowning.
They hit me when I was down,
but GOD stuck by me
He stood me up on a wide-open field;
I stood there saved—surprised to be loved!
—Psalm 18:16–19

I am encouraged that this is not the last time the psalmist expressed desolation and described the consolation he received from God. Moving from desolation to consolation is a part of almost every psalm. As I navigate my relational realities, I know that desolation is inevitable. I will again feel hurt and abandoned. My choice to step on to the way of consolation is a choice to allow the pain to take me to God, to wait for his healing touch, and to let him take me to others with the good news that trusting in the care of God is the goal of our journeys.

> *When you cannot practice the presence of God, then it is something to practice the absence of God.*
>
> —C. S. Lewis, *The Four Loves*

The Paralysis of Pain, the Protection of God

Daily and difficult relationships can leave us immobilized because we are stuck in the mundane or are paralyzed because the pain is not what we expected, doesn't make sense, is too intense, and doesn't seem like it will ever go away. In his profound book on suffering, Mike Mason writes, "Pure suffering has a consciousness, a tongue, a heart all of its own, and even the memory of it is but a pale unreality when compared with the actual experience. Only the sufferer himself, in the moment of piercing torment, knows what it is really like, and his knowing is a sort that drastically alters the very meaning of the verb 'to know.' "⁴Mason's poignant description of pain reveals why it can be so paralyzing. When we are "in the moment of piercing torment," it's hard to believe we can move, much less know where to move.

In the middle of my "tunnel-walking days" of pain (those are the days when you can barely put one foot in front of the other because the darkness engulfs you and the pain is so intense) after the breakup of my marriage, I went to the Midwest for a monthlong retreat. I didn't expect it to make much of a difference. During the second week, I began to drag myself out of bed to go for a morning walk and continue my practice of coming to God. I walked among the tall pines of the Minnesota forest and tried to swat away as many mosquitoes as I could. I was coming to God, but I was angry and could not see why he would allow me to be in such a vulnerable, painful, seemingly unprotected place in my life. One morning, I spotted a deer about a hundred feet in front of me. Since I'm a city girl, I'm a little afraid of wildlife. I stopped and waved my arms around, trying to shoo the deer away, but it stood fast. It didn't take long for me to give up, turn around, and jog back the way I'd come. When I looked back over my shoulder, I couldn't believe my eyes. The deer seemed to be charging me! I ran as fast as I could without looking back again. As I collapsed on my bed, I wailed about everything in my life that wasn't working. "Even the deer are chasing me!" I cried out to God.

The next morning, I gathered up my courage and ventured out on the same path. I slowed down when I came to the bend in the road where I had seen the deer the day before. There was no deer in sight. I continued on the path, up a little hill, and saw—exactly at the spot adjacent to where the deer had stood—a half eaten baby deer in the middle of the road. The shocking sight propelled me to jog by even faster, but I couldn't get the gruesome scene out of my mind. As I continued on the path, I realized that the day before, the deer hadn't been chasing me; it had been standing guard, protecting its baby. During the night, the mother deer's protection somehow hadn't been enough, and the baby was killed by predators. In the moment when I encountered the dead baby deer on the path, God broke through my pain and whispered, "Sharon, I haven't been allowing these things in your life because I'm not watching very closely. I've been protecting you, longing to keep you from ending up half eaten, lying dead in the middle of the road." Protecting me? Could I believe that in the midst of incomprehensible relational realities, God was actually protecting me from further harm and danger that I couldn't see? In that moment, I surrendered. I surrendered my pain and my paralysis to a God who can do a far better job of protecting me than I can. What a relief! I no longer needed to strive to figure everything out. In the midst of the inexplicable, I decided to believe that God was protecting me. Since I didn't need to be in charge, I could listen to instruction from others, read God's Word with a belief that it was a love letter to me, and rest in knowing that I didn't need to find a way to make my world work.

Learning to trust in God's protection requires that we give up our image of what protection is. We tend to believe that protection means we will experience no harm or hardship. Trusting God's protection compels us to accept harm and hardship not only as a context in which God cares for us but also as a place of protection. We must come to believe that God's care is more real than our pain and that his protection is active even when we cannot see it. Since the breakup of my marriage, I have come to believe that God has been protecting me all along—protecting me in the midst of my bad choices and from realities that I could not predict, chasing me over and over again to keep me from ending up half eaten in the middle of the road. Nothing has made this more clear than the evidence I have seen in lives of my children. The divorce certainly left them vulnerable to so many scary realities. My anger, depression, and relapse into alcoholism certainly didn't do much to add to their sense of safety and security. Over the years, I have tried to compensate for their hurt by doing all I could for them. I have worried and wondered how they would survive a broken family. It has taken a few years for me to trust that God was protecting my children even in the midst of their parents' foolish and potentially destructive choices.

A little over two years ago, on Easter Sunday, I tried all day long to reach my daughter by telephone. She was in her senior year of college in a city about two hours away. She didn't answer her phone all day. I continued to call until about 11:00 p.m. and then I sent her a text message, "I'm worried about you." Finally, she responded, "I'm sleeping." Her answer seemed strange to me, so I called her again. When she answered, she didn't sound at all like herself as she said, "Mom, I need help."

"What's wrong?" I answered as panic started to rise within me.

"I think I'm an alcoholic," she mumbled.

"You can't be an alcoholic," I said, as I stopped in my tracks. "You don't even drink. I'm an alcoholic. You've seen me. *You are not an alcoholic.*"

"Mom, I've been drinking for a while. I really started drinking a lot when I was traveling on Semester at Sea last semester. I drink more than anyone I know. It's starting to get me into trouble ..." Her voice faded off, and I could hear her crying.

I started to cry too. "Honey, can you just go to sleep, and we'll talk about it tomorrow?" She agreed.

I spent the rest of the night raging at God. How could this happen? This is the last thing that I wanted for my daughter. I had begged God to protect her from this disease that had cost me so much. How could he have failed? A collage of images flooded my mind: the divorce, my relapse, my daughter's pain and frantic efforts to stay busy in her own life so that she would not be touched by the pain in mine. Once again my heart shrank as I wondered how God could be trusted in all of this.

The next morning, Kristin drove home and told me her story of drinking. We both cried a lot and looked at each other in bewilderment. I asked if she would go to an Alcoholics Anonymous meeting. She agreed. By the end of that first day, she told her dad and brother and emailed all of her friends that she thought she was an alcoholic. On returning to school, she immediately started attending Twelve Step meetings. She got a sponsor and started to work the steps.

Kristin has been sober for more than two years. Just this week I got to hear her tell her story at an AA meeting. After the meeting, I sat at the back of the room while tears streamed down my face. I watched my daughter talk with many fellow strugglers who approached her. I overheard one woman say, "I have heard a lot of people speak about their alcoholism, but I have never heard anyone speak so passionately about their relationship with God!"

At that moment, it was as if I had put on glasses and could see clearly for the first time! I saw the divorce, my relapse in front of my children, my desperation for help, and my participation in a support group—I saw all of these things forming a hedge of protection around my dear daughter, because God has used all of these things to bring Kristin into a radical reliance on him. In a way that I could have never invited or orchestrated, God was protecting Kristin not only from getting lost in alcoholism but ultimately from drifting away from him.

We learn to look for the protection of God when we remember the ways that he has cared for us in the past and we become willing to wait for his way to unfold. The words of theologian F. B. Meyer challenge and convict me to wait for eyes to see more clearly before I throw my hands up, despairing that God can't be trusted: "All this is under the direction of a wise and faithful love, which is educating you for a glorious destiny. Believe only that your circumstances are those most suited to develop your character. They have been selected out of all possible combinations of events and conditions, in order to effect in you the highest finish of usefulness and beauty; *they would have been the ones selected by you, if all the wide range of omniscient knowledge had been within your reach.*"[5]

What are the inexplicable events in your relational life that tempt you to believe that God is silent or that trap you in the paralysis of pain? Are you willing to believe that these are the experiences that God wants to use to care for you and protect you? Being willing to trust in the care and protection of God is the beginning of experiencing his care and protection. Trusting God's care and protection can feel risky because we need to let go of the illusion that we are in control. Can you trust that everything that has happened to you was necessary to bring you to this moment, a moment when you want to trust him more than you want to be in control or figure things out?

> *God is keeping careful watch over us and the future. The Day is coming when you'll have it all — life healed and whole.*
>
> —1 Peter 1:5

The Pit of Despair, the Rescue of God

We can come to believe in the care of God and develop faith that frees us from the paralysis of pain yet still be bogged down with despair. Because we are designed to find life in, and to give life to, relationships, our energy for relationships becomes depleted when our relationships are lost, broken, disappointing, or difficult. We are in the pit of despair when we no longer have the energy to be active in the life of love. We stop hoping, risking, creating, forgiving, praying, beginning again, and believing again in relationships. We go through the motions, do our duty, and collapse at the end of the day with little hope for more. Friends may see our lethargy and encourage us to take an antidepressant, join a support group, or sign up for an internet dating service, but if all relational pain gets us back to God, then we need *him* to rescue us from the pit of spiritual despair (that's what a lack of trust is). Spiritual despair is a kind of "hunger strike" that says, "If you don't give me what I was made for, I quit—I give up!" When we are in the pit, sometimes we can't see his face of mercy, welcome, and kindness. We can't set ourselves free; we must be set free. We must be rescued.

I waited patiently for the LORD;
he turned to me and heard my cry.
He lifted me out of the slimy pit,
out of the mud and mire;
he set my feet on a rock
and gave me a firm place to stand.

—Psalm 40:1–3 NIV

God's rescue seldom seems like rescue in the beginning. After all, this is the God who rescued the baby Moses by sending him floating down a muddy river in a basket-cradle. He used a slingshot and a few rocks to rescue David from a giant named Goliath. He rescued Esther through a beauty pageant and the genocidal plotting of a wicked government official. God used famine, plagues, and a lifelong walk through the wilderness in his grand plan to rescue the Israelites. He rescued a prostitute, Rahab, with a scarlet cord in her window on a dangerous night, and she went on to become a prominent figure in the human lineage of Christ. Throughout the New Testament, God rescues the poor and outcast through the message and miracles of Jesus, and then he rescues us all with the scandal of a crucifixion and the unbelievable surprise of a resurrection. As the writer of Hebrews reflects, "I could go on and on ... They were protected from lions, fires, and sword thrusts, turned disadvantage to advantage, won battles, routed alien armies. Women received their loved ones back from the dead. There were those who, under torture, refused to give in and go free, preferring something better: resurrection" (Heb. 11:32–35).

We come to believe in God's care, protection, and rescue as we begin to believe in something better than our present circumstances: that difficult and painful relationships are the path to seeing God, not just with our eyes but with our hearts. We cannot trust others until we trust God, and most often we are compelled to need God—I mean really need him—only when others fail us. We can't trust ourselves—that we will be able to navigate relationships even if they fail and falter again—unless we trust God, and most often we throw ourselves completely on God only when we come to the end of ourselves. Do you see what that means? The broken, painful, lonely, shattering realities of relationships are part of the rescue. We begin to trust again, even when we are in the pit of despair, when we look at the painful realities of our lives and wonder how God is going to use those very realities to rescue us. As we wonder, we begin to look for God's protection, and while we are looking, we discover that he is already at work to rescue us.

I experienced the rescue of God with a private sign that was viewed by millions of people. During those two dark years after my marriage broke apart completely, I hardened my heart to any idea of forgiveness. Forgiveness of others requires that I trust God. I can forgive only to the degree that I know I am loved and have been forgiven. I can forgive only if I believe that God can be trusted with my heart and with others in my life, especially others who have hurt me. I had no interest in forgiving my ex-husband. My friends didn't want me to forgive him. My parents didn't want me to forgive him. My lawyer certainly didn't want me to forgive him. Every time my pastor preached on forgiveness, I turned to a friend and said, "I'm not going to forgive him," and she wisely responded, "You don't have to." Even though my hard heart kept me trapped in the pit of despair, I didn't want to get out. I needed to be rescued.

God's rescue came in the United Artists Meadows 12 movie theater. I was watching *Bruce Almighty*, a movie that I thought would be a comedy. I did laugh a lot during the movie, though I also winced as the main character made a mess of his life and world when he tried to be God. But it was the ending that caught me completely off guard. Bruce prays for his estranged girlfriend, Grace. He prays that Grace will be loved as she deserves to be loved and will always be seen the way he sees her now—through the eyes of a caring God. Bruce goes back to his old life with a new heart, and everywhere he sees signs of grace.

Without warning, I felt compelled to pray, "Oh God, I want to pray for my ex-husband that way." I believe that God simply answered, "Okay." And I began to forgive. It didn't happen overnight and I haven't done it perfectly, but on most days, I pray those words for my ex-husband, and that prayer is rescuing me from the pit of bitterness and resentment.

Well, it's just a silly movie. Or is it? When we come to believe that whatever the story, God wants to use it to romance us to *his* love and *his* longing, then he can fill our emptiness with love, forgiveness, and healing. Our stories and pain are real. Or are they? When we learn to look for something more real—the care, protection, and rescue of God—we can trust again. We won't trust all the time or trust perfectly, but we can face life on life's terms, and instead of languishing in the pit of despair and shuddering, "I can't trust anyone!" we can get up every morning and cry out, "Lord Jesus, I trust you, help my lack of trust."

Trusting again—in the care of God, the protection of God, and the rescue of God—begins with acknowledging honestly how you have felt uncared for, unprotected, and abandoned. As you reflect on those experiences, what do you want most? Justice? Revenge? A guarantee that you'll never be hurt again? Or do you want to become a woman of faith? I doubt that any of us would say that we want to become a woman of doubt, resentment, and bitterness. Daring to trust again is the path out of anger and despair and toward becoming a woman characterized by rest, forgiveness, and mercy. This week tell God about the experiences that make you feel hurt and abandoned. Ask for his comfort and wait for it; don't harden your heart if relief doesn't come quickly. When you feel the pain of relational distress, can you trust that the pain is a cue for you to remember that you don't see the whole picture? Ask God for the faith to trust that he is up to something more than what you can see. And when you feel your heart whimpering, "I just want someone to take care of me, to rescue me from loneliness, confusion, or heartache," can you trust that God's rescue is always intended to take us into a relationship with him? Are you willing to want that rescue more than you want resolution in any human relationship?

Just for You

1. Try painting or drawing a picture first of desolation and then of the consolation of God. Use colors or shapes that reflect your own experience of abandonment and comfort. You might want to cut out pictures or words to make a collage that reflects your experience of desolation or consolation.

2. Spend some time reading the Psalms. Note the psalmist's progression from desolation to consolation.

3. Think of an experience that eroded your trust in others. How did that experience impact your ability to trust God?

4. Reflect on how you physically experience a lack of trust in relationships. Do your shoulders stiffen? Do you feel anxiety in the pit of your stomach? How do you emotionally experience a lack of trust? Do you withdraw in tense conversations? Do you ever let people see you cry? How do you think your physical and emotional responses affect others?

5. Who do you depend on for comfort, direction, or support during relational difficulties? If you don't depend on others, how does your self-reliance affect you and your relationships?

6. Has there been a time in your life when God seemed silent? How did you respond?

7. How do you come to God with your relational pain? What stops you from coming to God?

8. Have you ever felt abandoned by God but later discovered that he was protecting you?

9. How have the difficulties in relationships led you to know God more deeply and depend on him more radically?

CHAPTER EIGHT

Living in Hope Again

Hope is a dangerous thing.

—Ellis Boyd "Red" Redding,
Shawshank Redemption

MY FRIEND DOTTIE SITS on her front porch every morning between 5:30 and 6:00 a.m. Sometimes she holds a Bible. Other times her head is bowed and her lips move as she prays, or maybe she's just talking to herself. Dottie lives only a mile from my house, and many mornings, I drive by her front porch on my way to get a cup of coffee. Occasionally, I stop and join her in her morning vigil. I have found her holding a photo album, flipping through pictures, traveling in her mind to places and times far away from her porch. Once I found her sitting in her rocking chair with tears streaming down her face. I sat down on the stool next to her, and she reached over and held my hand. We didn't say anything.

I wouldn't know what to say. Dottie's firstborn son left home when he was seventeen years old. He was mad at his father because he felt he constantly criticized him and wanted him to live up to an unrealistic and unwanted agenda. He went to the West Coast, and Dottie didn't hear from him for three years. When he finally called home, he told his mom that he was living in a commune, living off the land, and living with his girlfriend, who was pregnant with his child. He ended the short conversation by saying, "Mom, I love you. Don't tell Dad I called." Dottie couldn't have told her husband if she wanted to. Six months earlier, he had died in his sleep of a massive heart attack. She might also have told her son, if she'd had the chance, that she had recently been diagnosed with ovarian cancer.

Dottie got a Christmas card this year from her son, postmarked in California. The take-control, private-detective, make-something-happen part of me urged Dottie to hire an investigator to find her son. She asked, "Well, what would I do when I find him?"

"Tell him to come home, tell him that his father has died, that you miss him and need him, and that you want to be a part of your grandbaby's life!" I imagined joining Dottie as we trekked through some remote part of California's mountains or desert, arriving with baby clothes from Gymboree, snacks from Whole Foods for her son, and Aveda bath and beauty products for his girlfriend. I just knew that we could *make* a reconciliation happen by showing up with the best products that civilization has to offer, and if that didn't work, I wouldn't have a problem "guilting" her son into coming home to help take care of his mom.

My friend responded to my plan with a gentle smile and a real-life twinkle in her eyes, "My hope isn't in a private investigator, a surprise party, stuff from the mall, my most congenial words of invitation to relationship, or even any guilt trip you might invite him to!"

"Well what are you hoping for?" I asked, a bit disappointed that we wouldn't be embarking on this search and rescue.

"I hope for God," Dottie said.

"Hope for him to do what?" I wanted an action plan, a to-do list, and a foreseeable outcome for God, Dottie, and her son.

"I hope for him to meet me in the morning, to fill me with who he is, and to remind me of who I am. I hope to live out of our morning rendezvous all day long." Dottie smiled at me and then asked if she could join me on my trip to Starbucks.

For over a year, I have watched Dottie "put feet" to her hope every morning by faithfully showing up on the porch for prayer and meditation. I join her on her porch as often as I can, even if it's for only a few minutes. I try to borrow some of her hope and ask God to remind me of who he is, because I know that when I forget who he is, I forget who I am, and then I live in a hopeless morass of trying to plan, fix, manage, control, and push my way into hope.

The ABCs of Hope

Dottie has taught me what I have come to call the ABCs of hope. She has taught me, day after day after day, how to *Accept* what I cannot change. I have watched her accept the distance and the unknown in her relationship with her son as she settles in to ask God to be the source of her hope. Some days I get to *Be* with Dottie in her daily hope transfusion as she turns her face toward God, praying, "Give me this day, my daily hope." And I have watched her *Choose* hope in her relationship with her son, choices that have involved espionage, adventure, and great risk (I'll tell you about that later!). Accept. Be. Choose. These are the ABCs of hope.

Disappointment, estrangement, loss, heartbreak, and confusion in relationships do not need to extinguish hope. The ABCs of hope can guide us into living with hope again, but as Red in the movie *Shawshank Redemption* warns: "Hope is a dangerous thing. Hope can drive a man [or woman] insane." When we move toward living with hope again, we know in the depths of our being that we are risking feeling again all the hurt and heartache that we've experienced in relationships before. After our hope falls through the cracks of a broken or breaking life, we can identify with the words of the Weeping Prophet, Jeremiah: "I gave up on life altogether. I've forgotten what the good life is like. I said to myself, '... God is a lost cause.'... I'll never forget the trouble, the utter lostness, the taste of ashes, the poison I've swallowed. I remember it all— oh, how well I remember—the feeling of hitting the bottom" (Lam. 3:17–20).

Remembering can keep us feeling utterly lost, tasting the ashes of dead hopes and dreams, and giving up on life. The prophet goes on to describe the life that can come when we allow our remembrances to include more than our painful experiences: "But there's one other thing I remember, and remembering, I keep a grip on hope: God's loyal love couldn't have run out" (Lam. 3:21–22). Dottie had lost her son, her husband, and her grandchild, but her hope hadn't run out because she had discovered a morning ritual that allowed her to keep a grip on hope.

I think about Dottie almost every day—when I feel hopeless that I will ever know romance, companionship, or even a date again; when I doubt that my children will live out of faith fully rooted in God through Christ Jesus; when I worry about my aging parents; when I wonder if my friends even care that I am almost fifty years old, much less if they will think of throwing me a birthday party for this half-century occasion; when I fret that I will never get out of debt or be able to stop working; when the arthritis in my knee taunts me with all the other "it's downhill from here" physical realities that I will inevitably face in the next years; or even when I can't find one single pair of jeans in my closet that comfortably fits me.

On all of these occasions, it helps me to recall Dottie's morning meeting with hope. I remember that hope isn't found in a spouse or a romance or even a date, it isn't found in children who grow up and do everything God's way, and it isn't found in the number of one's friends, in full bank accounts, or in youthful, size 6 bodies. In fact, without hope, all of those things can be pretty empty. Novelist Pearl Buck poignantly observed, "To eat bread without hope is still to slowly starve to death."[1] I have experienced that even if I have a marriage, wonderful children, lots of friends, financial security, and a size 6 body and still lose hope, which is to lose God, then I lose myself. I am grateful for Dottie; in rain, snow, or sunshine, she sits on her porch and models to me the ABCs of hope.

Suddenly you will [know] that the petrifying visage of hopelessness is only God's rising in your soul.

—Karl Rahner,
The Need and the Blessing of Prayer

Accept

"Acceptance is the answer to *all* my problems today."[2] This is one of the most maddening sentences I have ever read in the *Big Book* of Alcoholics Anonymous. Sometimes I have shouted out loud, "You just don't know how big my problems are! What are you saying? I should just be okay with everything that is hurting, frustrating, and confusing me?" Simply put, acceptance is acknowledging our present reality and refusing to attach confining emotions to it. The most redemptive definition of *acceptance* is "a long and loving look at what really is." I can accept that I am lonely, but that doesn't mean I am unloveable and will never experience companionship. We can accept a failure in a relationship without concluding that we are worthless. I can accept that someone has hurt me, but I don't need to conclude that they or I am hopeless. Acceptance allows acknowledgement of everything that we've done and that's been done to us but keeps us from concluding with despair that we or others are hopeless, worthless, or unloveable. Acceptance allows us to acknowledge what is and to discover our need for God in that reality. Acceptance makes room for every experience and for God's presence.

I am learning that acceptance makes room for hope. I am learning this essential truth by simply practicing acceptance. I have discovered that the only reality more difficult than accepting the inexplicable is railing against it. When I am in the anguish of not accepting, my pain, outrage, and frantic scrambling don't leave any room for hope. Acceptance says, "I accept this painful, confusing, unjust reality. I don't know what to do. I trust God, or I want to trust God." That simple statement is the answer to whatever the problem is today. Surrendering to what is and to God may not solve anything. We may need to do something. We may need someone else to do something. We may need a miracle from God. But until we accept our present reality, there is no room for any positive solution.

I have a dear friend who is going through the heartbreaking trauma of infidelity in her marriage. She doesn't know what to do. Many friends say, "Throw the bum out." A few say, "Wait. If he repents, maybe you can build a new marriage." She has spent many mornings lying on her bed, raging at God and her husband, and wallowing in the hopelessness of not knowing what she should do. Several weeks ago, I read her the sentence on acceptance from the *Big Book*. She was initially confused, and then she was mad. "Am I just supposed to accept what he has done to me?" We talked through her anger and confusion until she was able to pray, "I accept that my marriage is broken. I don't know what to do. I want to rely on God to lead me." A few weeks later, she wrote this beautiful letter to her husband.

> What if?... What if I refused to go through with a divorce? What if I said that this family is not going to be destroyed? What if the body of Christ would gather around our family and as an entire body pray to take back the family out of the death grip of Satan? What if I could love you today and not worry about the pain that you might cause me tomorrow? What if I could love you today and not worry about the pain you have caused me yesterday? What if God doesn't show up with great miracles but expects and hopes that we might perform the miracles ourselves? What if I would allow the thought to occur that you are trying to be kind, that you are trying to find a way to live out your repentance? What if I could give you a chance? What does it mean to keep hanging on the cross? What does it mean to not worry about hanging on the cross? What does it mean to really die? What does it mean to really hope?

Acceptance made room for my friend to wonder about forgiveness, perseverance, kindness, risk, possibilities, crucifixion, and resurrection. Today I cannot tell you what is going to happen in her marriage, but I can tell you that her heart is beginning to be filled with hope, not hope in her husband or herself but hope that God is in the questions and the answers.

After the sentence about acceptance, the next sentence in the *Big Book* is, "Nothing, absolutely nothing, happens in God's world by mistake."[3] God doesn't cause affairs, abuse, or any of the infinite number of ways that we hurt ourselves and hurt each other, but his allowing them to happen is not a mistake. He hopes that all of the relational pain we experience will lead us to the end of human resources, to acceptance, and to the knowledge that he alone is hope. This is not some simplistic platitude. It is lived out by my friend Dottie, meeting God every morning on her porch and developing a real, intimate relationship with her Creator. It is experienced by my friend who is going through trauma in her marriage, as she cries out to God, looks for God, questions God, and desperately needs God to show up. Her doubt and despair demonstrate the presence of the sort of authentic relational faith that God always honors.

Be

Acceptance allows us to be in the moment, to be fully alive — no matter how painful or unwanted our circumstances might be — and to be aware, listening, and available for the next moment. Being still and simply *being* is the only reality that invites us to believe that we are loved with nothing asked in exchange, absolutely nothing. Our real identity depends on what we are, not on what we do. Being reminds us of who we were all along in Christ before we did anything right or wrong. It is hard to live in hope if I am consumed with the past or anxious about the future. Now, in case you are thinking that I sound really "Zen" and have attained some mystical state of being, let me confess that simply being is probably the hardest practice for me of any spiritual discipline. If you told me to read twelve books, memorize one chapter from each, take groceries to two families, do five loads of laundry, and run three miles, I would gladly take on those tasks over the practice of being. Being still doesn't seem practical or productive to me. I'm not even sure I really know how to do it, but I can share with you what I have learned about being still and how it has allowed me to live in hope again. When I accept that this present moment is all I have and devote myself to be in this moment, I can hear from God, I can give thanks for all that this one moment contains, and I am strengthened to step into the next moment.

Being requires returning to a Source that is deeper than ourselves and our human relationships. Each of us needs to find the spiritual exercise that helps us return to the Source of Life. I have learned that when I take the time to listen, I discover that God is with me. And I have learned not to be afraid of the silence if I don't hear from him immediately; while I wait to hear from God, I can give thanks. Giving thanks opens my spirit, so that I can hear more clearly from God, not with my head but with an open heart, and that allows me to see more clearly where

> *Be still, and know that I am God.*
>
> —Psalm 46:10 NIV

to go next. Living in hope is a constant journey, back and forth, between my inner life and my external relationships. As I listen and give thanks, hope grows within, so that I can move toward others in hope.

Listen

One morning I stopped by to see Dottie during her morning meditation. I did not feel meditative. I was filled with self-pity, loneliness, and anxiety. I am prone to depression, and it often creeps in and reminds me of everything in my life that is not the way that I wish it was, which tends to extinguish any hope I have. I identify with the words the poet Yeats used to describe his own prone-to-melancholy personality: he "had an abiding sense of tragedy which sustained [him] through temporary periods of joy."[4] I plopped down on Dottie's stool and said, "I'm just tired of being a lonely, vulnerable, anxious, needy, alcoholic, middle-aged woman!" Dottie laughed and invited me to join her every morning for the next two weeks on the porch.

"What am I supposed to do, bring, think about, pray, or read?" I asked. Dottie answered, "Just bring yourself. It sounds like you need this ritual to find hope again." She was right that I needed hope. I wasn't sure how a ritual of simply being could bring anything but restlessness and agitation to my uptight, always-on-the-go heart. During the first week, the thirty minutes seemed like thirty days. I had moments of peace or even insight, but I still found myself thinking about everything I needed to get done and everything in my life that was hopelessly undone.

By the second week, I was looking forward to my respite on the porch. The morning ritual felt kind of like a punctuation mark in my life that reminded me to pause. Slowly, I began to make friends with the silence, and as I experienced the grace of my own company, I discovered that I wasn't alone. On the final morning, my heart started to flutter with a sense that God saw me and was speaking to me. I heard him in that stillness in a way that I haven't often heard him. His Spirit communed with mine: "Don't be afraid. I have redeemed you. I have called you by your name and you are mine. You are precious in my eyes, because you are honored and I love you. The mountains may depart, the hills be shaken, but my love for you will never leave you, and my covenant of peace with you will never be shaken" (see Isaiah 54:4, 10). When I got home, I pulled out my journal and wrote what I knew he was speaking to me—lonely, vulnerable, anxious, needy, alcoholic, middle-aged me—in the stillness of being present:

Dear, dear Sharon,

I do see you this morning, and I see your entire story. Please believe that I am the grand storyteller of your life. You are not. I find your story interesting, painful, and heartbreakingly beautiful because it is the perfect story, you are the perfect story, for me to be telling.

You are not alone. I delight to call you "daughter." I am proud of who you are, not what you do. That means your strength and weakness, your generosity and anger, your gifts and inadequacies, your energy and weakness, your accomplishments and utter lostness. Yes, even when you are wandering in hopelessness and cannot find your way to your seat, I am proud to put my arm around you, gently lead you to your seat, sit beside you, and tell everyone, "This is my daughter!"

You are not hopeless. I know that in your heart and soul you believe that your story is too much for anyone. The truth is that I am too much for your story. I forgive you, heal you, renew you every day, and in the times when that is hardest to believe, you are dearest to me. You see, you need me.

You are not loverless. When you feel unwanted, instead of working so hard, will you seek my affection? When you are exhausted, can you risk laying down your head? And when you feel unworthy, oh, dear Sharon, will you believe that you are my bride? Bone of my bones. Flesh of my flesh. Please look at me. Just look at me. I will never be unfaithful to you. I will never divorce you. You are mine.

I guess that's really what I want you to hear this morning. I am yours. You are mine.

When we choose to simply *be*, we can hear words of hope. The words I heard that morning did not solve my problems or take away my painful realities, but they did remind me of the source of hope: "I am with you." When we open our hearts to God's being the only reality that offers life-changing, sustained hope, all of the difficulties and disappointments in our lives look different.

When was the last time you heard from God about who he

is in your life? Perhaps you haven't heard because you haven't practiced being still and listening. The Weeping Prophet kept a grip on hope when he remembered, "God's loyal love couldn't have run out, his merciful love couldn't have dried up. They're created new every morning" (Lam. 3:22–23). The practice of being still can allow hope to seep into our souls when we are willing to listen for God's love—not for answers, steps to take, or promises of health and wealth—but for God's loyal love. The prophet continued, "I'm sticking with God (I say it over and over)" (Lam. 3:24). We live in hope when we are still and hear

> *When life is heavy and hard to take, go off by yourself. Enter the silence. Bow in prayer. Don't ask questions: Wait for hope to appear.*
>
> —Lamentations 3:28–29

that God is sticking with us. His loyal love renews our commitment to stick with him (and yes, I have to say it over and over and over again). God sticks with us. We stick with him. *That is hope.*

Give Thanks

Being still and listening can be a challenge. I was blessed to have Dottie's encouragement and her modeling to me the practice of being still. Sometimes we can't quiet ourselves because our heads and hearts are full of people and problems. Other times we can't stay still because those same people and problems make too much noise for us to hear the "still, small voice." Giving thanks is the spiritual exercise that opens our hearts, quiets us in the moment, and allows us to hear God's voice. Giving thanks does not mean that people and problems go away. Gratitude does not come from a life in which we experience everything we thought we wanted. I used to believe that people were grateful because they had what they wanted. I have learned that when we are grateful, we want what we have. The practice of being still flourishes when we can be grateful in the moment.

I need help being grateful because hardships often leave me feeling entitled, so I recently did a little research to help me be grateful. This is how that research aided me in my practice of *being* today.

I went to bed last night feeling yucky. I know that's not a real feeling, but it best describes the mix of emotions that were bubbling up inside of me. I felt restless, irritable, and discontent. I had my reasons. I'd been misunderstood and judged by a friend. My car was leaking something in a puddle of pending trouble in my garage. A check I'd received as payment for work done bounced. I could go on, but you get the idea.

I woke up this morning remembering a commitment I made to myself while sitting in the silence of Dottie's porch: that I would spend moments of being thankful every day. I decided it might not be a bad idea to begin practicing this the first thing on this day since I was feeling a residue of yuckiness from the night before. As I reached for the light and turned off my alarm clock, I noticed that both worked predictably, with little effort from me. I recalled that 1.6 billion people in this world live without electricity and rely on burning wood, dung, and agricultural waste (which cause air pollution, one of the world's top ten causes of premature death). So I gave thanks for electricity and for not ever having to even think about dung when I turn on my light.

I always check my BlackBerry first thing in the morning. I know it's geeky and a little scary, but I love my BlackBerry. I even have nightmares about losing it. There might be an element of addiction there, and life might be less stressful if we weren't constantly connected to our telephones, but I'm grateful for my cell phone. Most people on earth live more than two hours from a telephone. Most places in the world do not have access to basic internet, and over one-quarter of the world's population is without postal service. I scrolled down the screen on my cell phone and noted the number of people I talked to yesterday, the one waiting voice mail, and several new email messages and gave thanks. I read a recent study about loneliness in the United States and remember feeling deep sadness at its finding: one-quarter of all Americans report that they have no one to talk to.

Then I used my bathroom. I remembered being in Cambodia a few years ago and needing to find a restroom on one of our drives across the country. I announced my need to our guide and casually offered, "It will be fine to just stop at a gas station." She quickly shook her head at my ignorant suggestion and explained, "Oh, no that would not be good. We will stop at a nice house and pay to use their bathroom." We finally found a house that she thought looked suitable, knocked on the door, and offered these strangers one dollar to use their outhouse, which had a clean dirt floor and a hole in the ground surrounded by wooden boards. Until my trip to this country, I hadn't known that over half of the world's population does not have toilets.

Next I turned on the water faucet (one of six in my home) to get a drink of water. A glass of clean water is never an option for one-quarter of the world's population, which is why more than two million people die every year from diseases they get from simply drinking water. With every sip, I gave thanks.

I laced up my Nikes and stepped outside for my morning run. As always, the sun was rising. I thought about some words a dear friend had sent me via email (which I read on my BlackBerry with my laser-corrected vision): "The world is full of resurrections. . . . Every night that folds us up in darkness is a death; and those of you, my friends, that have been out early, and have seen the first dawn, will know it—the day rises out of the night like a being that has burst its tomb and escaped into life."[5] I took in the sunrise and prayed, "Thank you for another resurrection."

And then I turned on my iPod to listen to music, music that fills me with joy, faith, and always hope. To think that sixteen out of every thousand people in the United States have a severe hearing impairment makes me grateful that I can hear the words and the melody coming from a miraculous, three-inch device that contains all my favorite songs. As I ran, I contemplated the day ahead: a day off from work for me! Because I am a bit prone to workaholism, I said a prayer for the 12 percent of all Americans who work seven days a week and asked for the grace to rest.

When I finished my exercise, I jumped in the car, which seemed to run fine even with the mysterious leak, and drove to a neighborhood café for coffee and a bagel. My heart overflowed with gratitude as I savored every bite of a pumpkin bagel slathered with peanut butter. I will never forget the pictures I saw of families in Haiti performing their daily ritual of making cookies from dirt, salt, and vegetable shortening. The cookies are their entire meal.

It only took being present to everything contained in one hour of my day to confirm that I have a lot to be grateful for. In fact, my ability to write these words on my six-year-old Compaq laptop computer and your ability to read them in the miracle of a book confirms that we are in the top 25 percent of the richest people in the world!

No matter how much my relationships don't work, when I am present to all that is contained in even one hour and give thanks, I am overflowing with hope. Being allows me to hear God and give thanks, which is the best starting point for the next step.

Step into the Next Moment

As much as I would have liked to spend my day sitting on Dottie's porch, listening to God, and giving thanks, one thing or another always pulled me off the porch, down the steps, and into the rest of my day with real relationships and real problems. I quickly noted the difference in my days when I spent a few moments being still compared to the days when I jumped out of bed and right into my to-do list. The practice of being allowed me to reflect on my day and make choices from a place of peace. Conversely, the practice of doing energized choices that were reactions rather than reflections and that often came from a place of turmoil. When I step into the next moment with a reaction to something that happened in previous moments, I am almost guaranteed to have a shortsighted and self-protective pattern of relating. When I can step into the next moment with reflection, I can offer my truest self to the situation and can have a vision for the future that is dependent on God, not me.

Thank God no matter what happens. This is the way God wants you who belong to Christ Jesus to live.

—1 Thessalonians 5:18

For over a year, Dottie has kept her appointment with hope. She has listened to God in the stillness of morning after morning. Her life of gratitude is evident to everyone she meets and spills over into her community. She writes thank-you cards to people for no reason, she delivers flowers from her garden to everyone in her neighborhood, and she visits people just for the fun of it. These are all expressions of the hope that fills her every morning. A few weeks ago when I stopped in to see Dottie, her face was beaming unusually brightly. She announced, "I'm ready to visit my son!" I asked a lot of questions, expressed my joy at Dottie's anticipated journey, and invited myself on the trip to the West Coast.

Dottie declined my offer to go with her and explained that she had received a phone call from her son two nights ago. He told her where he lived, and when she asked if she could come for a visit, he answered, "I could meet you in Santa Barbara and we could have dinner."

"That's all?" I was incredulous, "He expects you to fly out there to have dinner? What a selfish, thoughtless man!"

Dottie wasn't shaken. "Oh, Sharon, don't you see this is what I've been hoping for?"

Well, actually, I didn't see. "What do you mean?" I asked. "This doesn't seem that hopeful. It seems like he's asking a lot from you and not offering much in return."

"Oh, I haven't been hoping for anything from him. I have been hoping in God—hoping that he would guide me, hoping that he would give me a chance to share about his loyal love with my son, and hoping that through it all I would keep hoping in him." Then Dottie jumped up from her chair on the porch, saying, "Let me show you what I'm taking with me," and motioned for me to follow her into the house.

I had no idea what Dottie had prepared for her son, but I knew that she was ready to take this step. She wasn't taking it in resentment or with a need to make things work. I sensed no anger or desperation, and I knew that whatever she was bringing, it would not include guilt or manipulation. Dottie's practice of *being* on the porch filled her with hope, and that hope strengthened her to take the next step.

I thought of all the times in my messy relationships when I haven't waited for anything. Rather than reflecting on all that could be going on beneath the surface of a difficult relationship, I have reacted out of anger, hurt, and resentment. I have told people a thing or two, I have let them know everything that they have done wrong, and the only place to which I have invited them is to guilt and shame. I have responded to broken relationships not with hope but with me—my pain, my agenda, my unmet needs, and my sense of how things ought to be. I wondered if I would be willing to wait (Dottie had been waiting for over three years) for hope to grow in me before I stepped into the mess to offer an invitation to work on this difficult relationship again. Dottie's choices about her relationship with her son came from acceptance and being, practices that allowed hope to guide her to take the next step.

> *Can a man lay a new foundation every day? If he works hard, he can lay a new foundation at every moment.*
>
> —Abba Sylvanus,
> *The Paradise of the Holy Fathers*

Choose

We are at risk of making choices out of selfishness or manipulation when our choices are based on anything but hope. For example, in Dottie's broken relationship with her son, she could have simply said, "Fine. I'm just going to take care of myself. If he doesn't confess his wrong and repent, then I'm not going to allow him back in my life." That would be a selfish choice. A choice for self that does not hope for the other leaves us feeling guilty. Guilt and hope cannot grow at the same time. Dottie could just as easily have said, "When he calls me, I will apologize for everything and offer him money or a ticket to come visit, whatever he needs, just so we can be in relationship again." Of course, that potentially manipulative choice could easily lead to a sense of being taken advantage of, and resentment would grow. Resentment certainly chokes out hope.

We do need to make choices in our relational difficulties, and those choices will inevitably involve something that is for us and something that is for others. Either choice can kill hope if our motivation is to try to get what we want. Either choice can inspire greater hope if our deepest desire is to find a way—in the midst of our relational difficulties—for others and for ourselves to choose God. At this point, we don't need to prove ourselves or protect ourselves anymore. When we choose from this God-centered perspective, we are free because we are tethered to a relationship that is far more reliable and rewarding than human relationships.

Choosing for Ourselves in Hope

Sometimes it is necessary to take a break from a toxic relationship, and sometimes we have no choice but to allow loved ones in our lives to move away from us. When our only motive for a choice in relationships is to take care of ourselves, we inevitably will battle guilt. God created us for relationships so that we no longer have to live only for ourselves. The desire to think of, care for, and pay attention to another is woven into the fabric of our souls. Taking a break from a relationship, taking time to care for ourselves, or paying attention to our own needs will cause us to lose hope if we are doing these just to satisfy ourselves.

Taking a break from a relationship for the purpose of growing in our faith, hope, and love and hoping that in our absence, the other person will be drawn to the presence of God, is a choice for hope. When we care for ourselves so that we can care for others, that too is about hope. We've all learned this from the preflight instructions on an airplane. The flight attendants instruct us that if the plane is going down and we need oxygen, we should put on our own masks first so that we can then save our child who is flying with us. The airlines know that there is greater hope that we will be able to help others if we save ourselves first. When we pay attention to our own needs, we can make decisions about self-care, but more important, we will be able to recognize our unmet needs and surrender them to Jesus.

When I notice that I have unmet needs for companionship, security, and significance and determine to satisfy those needs at all costs, I will become frustrated, exhausted, and ultimately hopeless. When I instead choose to surrender my unmet needs to Jesus, those vulnerable places in my life become a place (like Dottie's porch) where I can spend time with God, fellowshiping together about who he is and who I am and how we can make this sometimes achingly painful journey together. That's a choice for hope.

In the brokenness of her relationship with her son, Dottie's choice was to care for herself in her daily ritual on the porch. She explained to me that while she spent all those hours on the porch praying for her son, she accepted that he was in God's hands. She also confessed to me, "Oh, Sharon, many mornings I prayed honestly, 'God, make him call me *today*. Let me get a letter. Show me in a vision where he is. Please, just make him show up on my doorstep, like in those Hallmark television commercials!'" Dottie went on to explain about her prayers of acceptance: "But then at the end of every prayer with all my requests, wishes, fantasies, and great ideas, I would simply say, 'God, he is in your hands.'" Accepting what's true in our relationships, who we are, and who God is gives us hope. Dottie has taught me that it is possible to choose for others and for ourselves in hope.

Choosing for Others in Hope

Many times when we are in messy, painful relationships, we reach out to others because we think it's the right thing to do, the Christian thing to do, or because it's something that we just have to do. That is not a course of action that grows out of hope. Choosing for others—to care and support them—just because it's the right thing to do makes us moralistic. Choosing for others without hope can become manipulative.

Many times I have done something for others because I felt it was the right thing to do and then ended up being filled with resentment and self-pity because they didn't respond as I thought they should. I didn't wait to grow into acceptance. I didn't do the hard work of being still and hearing from God. I wasn't present so that I could hear God's voice in the moment, so every next step I took was my own idea. That's a risky way to move in difficult relationships. Only when we wait to hear from God, keeping our hearts open with gratitude, can we discern his direction for the next step. It comforts me to know that he not only knows my heart but also knows the heart of the other party. I may be ready to move or take action, but the other person may not be. Being still allows me to follow the lead of the One who knows both hearts. Then when I choose to care for another, I can speak powerfully and move confidently because I genuinely want the well-being of the other and trust that God has prepared him or her for this moment. As Dottie cared for herself in her daily morning meditation, she gained clarity about how to care for her son in hope—a hope that strengthened her to risk loving even if there might be a cost.

I followed Dottie into her bedroom, where she had two packed suitcases on her bed. One was filled with her clothes and necessities. The other was filled with bundles wrapped in thick newspapers. I thought that perhaps Dottie had taken my suggestion and had gone to the mall to buy treats for her son.

Dottie pulled one bundle out of her suitcase and explained, "This is what I heard God tell me to do one morning while I was sitting on the porch." Dottie unwrapped a jar. I knew that it was some kind of food, but since I'm the queen of take-out,

I couldn't have guessed what homemade concoction might be in that jar. Dottie went on to tell me about the process of being still and listening to God. She thought about her son and her grandbaby living so far away. When she began to be filled with worry and questions about their well-being, she gave thanks that they were living in an environment that valued health and holistic living. She did some research on "living off the land" and discovered that it often meant growing organic food. Dottie took a class in organic gardening and in her suitcase was the fruit of her labor: canned beans, squash, and stewed tomatoes.

Tears welled up in my eyes as I looked at my friend. Her acceptance and practice of being—listening to God and cultivating gratitude—gave her hope. She had planted that hope, watered it, and prepared it to give to her son and his family.

This morning as I was making my daily drive to Starbucks, I saw Dottie sitting on her front porch. I swerved over to park in her driveway and ran to the porch anticipating a beautiful reunion story between mother, son, and grandbaby, with organic vegetables surrounding them!

"How did it go?" I asked enthusiastically.

"It was good," Dottie said, subdued. "He didn't bring the baby. They aren't ready for me to meet him yet. I told him about his dad and my cancer. He cried. He told me a lot about their life, but he was guarded and quite honestly, it was a little awkward.

"I asked him if he would come to visit, and he said he didn't know." I felt my disappointment growing. This was not the happy ending I wanted for Dottie. I thought of all the women I know who try so hard to accept difficulties in their lives, spend time being present to God and his gifts in their lives, and risk again in relationships. I wanted Dottie's story to be the story that would tell us all that *it works*.

"Oh Dottie, I'm so sorry. What are you going to do now?" I asked.

"I guess I'm just going to keep spending my morning time on the porch remembering who God is, who I am, and trying to live out of that each day." We were both quiet for a while, and then Dottie said, "What's the alternative, Sharon?" I sensed peace wrapped around her question.

I knew what she meant. To rage against our painful relational realities, to scramble to make life work, and to make choices for ourselves or others out of our hardened, frantic hearts kills hope. And without hope, we will slowly starve to death.

Accept. Be. Choose. The ABCs of hope are not a formula for making life work. They are a way of living that keeps us connected to the Source of Life. Every relational difficulty can either kill hope or drive us to hope, and freedom slowly grows as we understand that hope is not dependent on our relationships working. It is not dependent on us working. Hope is dependent solely on our wanting him. The more difficult and frustrating our relationships are, the more opportunities we have to want him. And the more we want him, the more we hope. "Not only so, but we also rejoice in our sufferings, because we know that suffering produces perseverance; perseverance, character; and character, hope. And hope does not disappoint us, because God has poured out his love into our hearts by the Holy Spirit, whom he has given us" (Rom. 5:3–5 NIV).

Just for You

1. What do you hope for from God? How do you "put feet" to your hopes? For example, if you hope for a romantic relationship, do you pray about it, ask others to pray about it, ask others to introduce you to their friends, take a class where you might meet someone with common interests?

2. What relational reality do you have a hard time accepting? Why? Consider entrusting it to God (over and over and over again) until you experience the rest of acceptance. Perhaps you can establish a ritual (like Dottie's morning time on her porch) in which you journal about the relationship, read the words out loud to God, and then envision handing the situation over to him.

3. Practice being still for fifteen minutes. What was the experience like for you? Did you hear anything during your time of listening? Consider maintaining this practice for at least a week. Write down what you hear from God as you practice *being* in his presence.

4. Dedicate one hour today to gratitude. During that hour, write down everything for which you can give thanks.

5. Can you think of a time when you responded to a messy relationship in hope? How did hope make a difference?

6. How can you choose to care for yourself in hope? In others words, as you practice self-care—a nap, a manicure, time reading and meditating, and so on—what are you hoping for?

7. Think back on a decision you made to do something for someone else. Did you offer to them out of duty or demand? What were you hoping for? How would you have acted differently if your hope for them was that they would know and want God more because of their interaction with you?

CHAPTER NINE

Falling in Love Again

These are moments of truth. You are alone with The Alone.... When the night is bad and my nerves are shattered and the waves break over the sides .... I have two choices. I can escape below into skepticism and intellectualism, hanging on for dear life. Or, with radical amazement, I can stay on deck and boldly stand in surrendered faith to the truth of my belovedness, caught up in the reckless raging fury that they call the love of God.

—Brennan Manning,
The Furious Longing of God

I AWOKE TO A series of popping sounds. I sat up, startled by the loud noises in what seemed to be the middle of the night (since I'm an early-to-bed person, 10:00 p.m. seems late!). I looked toward the front of my house and saw a flash of lights. It was unlikely that the sights and sounds meant gunshots and police cars, but I didn't know what in the world could be going on. I pulled on a sweatshirt and made my way down the stairs toward the front door. As I peeked through the blinds, it took a few moments for my brain to compute what I saw. Standing in my driveway were a client of mine and her husband. Judy is in her midsixties, and her husband, Bill, is seventy-eight years old. When I realized that they were standing in my driveway waving sparklers, I started to laugh. I rushed out to meet them, and Judy greeted me with a big hug as she continued to wave her sparkler above my head.

"What in the world are you doing?" I asked.

"I'm celebrating," she explained. "I have surrendered to the Story."

And then I knew. Judy is a woman of heroic proportions, living a story that she would have never chosen, and I knew that she had made a decision to see the theme of her story as love, even though her story at the moment was overwhelmingly confusing and painful.

An Unlikely Love Story

Judy had come to me for counseling about six months earlier when her husband of over forty years was diagnosed with Alzheimer's. She told me stories of Bill forgetting where his grown children lived or worked and of being unable to find the word for a familiar object. When Bill's cognitive decline could no longer be ignored, they began to see doctors and therapists. Judy spent hours reading the results of Bill's tests, researching medications available for the dreaded disease, and pleading with doctors that there had to be something more that they could do. Bill did begin a medication that eased Judy's anxiety for a bit, but it did not eradicate all of Bill's symptoms, and it became impossible for Judy to deny that she was slowly losing the man that she had loved for so many years.

Judy and I spent many hours together, talking about grief and suffering. She asked the inevitable question that all sufferers ask: Why? I never pretend to have an answer to that question, but I am coming to believe with greater certainty that the story behind every story is love. This conclusion may seem like a platitude when it is announced outside of suffering, but when it is believed in the midst of pain, it is evidence that a relationship with Jesus not only informs our thinking but at times overrides it.

When Judy and Bill lit sparklers in my driveway, it was Judy's way of announcing that she was choosing to surrender to the inexplicable truth that behind her story of pain and confusion was a love story. We talked about the faith required to believe that God was not looking down from heaven saying, "Good. Let her hurt. That will teach her." He was trying to teach her about love.

If that seems unthinkable to you, I understand your bewilderment. Judy's story reminds me that relationships set us up to experience pain, whether through loss, disease, sin, or failure. When we love someone, we always risk being hurt. In the midst of our pain, however, we are at risk of something far more deadly and dangerous than being hurt: the temptation to harden our hearts and determine that we will not be hurt again. We will not begin again or believe again. We will not love.

Our problem with desire is that we want too little.

—C. S. Lewis,
The Weight of Glory

Desire is the fuel of human relationships. It propels us to engage with others and with God. God made us hunger for relationships. When we determine to live without desire for relationship, we are more on the side of evil than of good. Although it can seem counterintuitive, when we are heartbroken, we stay on the healing path only when we surrender to falling in love again.

Surrender to the Story

It doesn't take something as overwhelming as Alzheimer's for us to harden our hearts to the vulnerability of surrendering to a story that's all about love. When we believe our story is only about tragedy, we surrender to a smaller story that doesn't make any sense at all. Even "paper cuts" that sting us in relationships can make us determine that we won't be hurt one more time, so we live in a smaller story of self-protection. Brokenness and betrayal in relationships have a way of absorbing all of our attention and distorting our perceptions so that we live in a pinched, paltry story of being a victim. The difficulties and disappointments in relationships can convince us that our story is a tragedy at worst and just filled with mistakes at best.

In the pages of this book, we have looked at surrender over and over again. We have considered surrendering our God-designed longing for relationships to our Designer, our brokenness to the Great Healer, our security and significance to the love of Christ, our humiliation to the humble King, our estranged relationships to the Crucified One, and our loneliness to the lonely God who, more than anything else, longs for a relationship with us. Every consideration of surrender is at heart an invitation to believe that every experience in human relationships is about one thing and one thing only: believing in the love of God. Daily and difficult relationships are intended to bring us to a place of abandon where we know, heart and soul, "What marvelous love the Father has extended to us! Just look at it ...! " (1 John 3:1).

Surrendering to the story of love is possible only when we tell the truth about love sought, love lost, love battered and broken, and love abandoned. And then we tell the story of Jesus, the One who came to seek and to find the lost, the One whose terrible, humiliating wounds heal us, the One whose love endures forever. The more we tell our stories in conjunction with his story, the more we become the story we are intended to tell, the more we become women who are loved when we are good for nothing, loved by the One who is simply good.

We may stumble on this path of surrender and may even step off the path, thinking that what we want is found in human relationships. When we experience the inevitable heartache in human relationships, it becomes an invitation to surrender again as we remember *the* story—that we are born again, renewed again, and healed again by the unfailing love of God. Surrender becomes a way of life when we believe that all relationships are about one thing only; they are invitations to *the* love story, our true story, the story that remains when all human realities shift, change, and even fail: we are the beloved of God. When we surrender to that story, we embrace him, and his embrace of us becomes more real than any relationship.

We need to be reminded to surrender over and over again, and there is nothing like relationships to prompt us to do so. The difficulties in relationships compel us to take charge, to give up, or to give in. The most beautiful surrender is when we give in, knowing that we are secure in the love of God. What does it mean to give in? We look for God, wait for him, watch for him, and want him in the midst of every human experience. We confess, rant, plead, listen, and talk to him. We tell him our stories. We read his stories. And when we are certain that we can't risk, pray, forgive, or try again, we ask him to help us begin again and to believe again in his love.

David describes surrender in Psalm 131, one of the shortest and loveliest psalms:

> My heart is not proud, O LORD,
>   my eyes are not haughty;
> I do not concern myself with great matters
>   or things too wonderful for me.
> But I have stilled and quieted my soul;
>   like a weaned child with its mother,
>   like a weaned child is my soul within me.
>
> —Psalm 131:1–2 NIV

A Shallow Story

While I was cleaning out closets this past spring, I came across a journal entry I wrote when I was a junior in high school. It describes the shallow story I was determined to live at the time. The cultural references will remind you that I am almost a half century old!

Mr. Right

"When you meet 'Mr. Right,' it may not be as exciting as television makes you believe," my mom chided as I described to her my dream man. I picture the perfect mate as a combination of Robert Redford and Bruce Jenner with the wealth of Howard Hughes. But most of all Mr. Right will be completely trustworthy. He will listen to the secrets of my heart and always be there to meet my needs. He will be absolutely consistent in his love for me. He will support me and be my biggest fan. His trustworthiness will not waver regardless of what I say or do. When I meet Mr. Right, I may discover that my mom is right and he won't be at all like the actors on television. But she is wrong about one thing—he will be exciting!

When I wrote those lines, I was surrendered to a story of a romance that would sweep me off my feet. I smile today knowing that Robert Redford is a grandfather, Bruce Jenner looks ridiculous due to some botched plastic surgery, and all of Howard Hughes' wealth did not follow him into the grave. Nevertheless, when my real-life story collided with my "happily ever after with Mr. Right" story, my life broke into a million little pieces and the foundation of my world crumbled. There is nothing like relational pain, heartbreak, and our uncovered voracious neediness to remind us of ourselves, and that often traps us in a vicious cycle of self-awareness and self-absorption. No place is lonelier than being stuck in our own disappointing and shallow story.

What keeps us mired in self-absorption and the inevitable loneliness and lovelessness that brings? I believe that the enemy of our souls relentlessly looks for something that will be more compelling, more absorbing, and more real than God, for he believes that finding that something will encourage us to harden our hearts to surrender and ultimately to love. Certainly, nothing is more compelling, more absorbing, and more real than our pain—than *ourselves*.

When my life becomes about me and my pain, I ensure that I won't get the one thing I want most, which is to love and be loved. As a sixteen-year-old, I didn't have a clue as to what I wanted most, and I certainly did not know that shattered dreams were the path to revealing my heart's true desire.

Our personal struggles are absurd and meaningless if we do not bear them with an open, surrendered heart. They become sacred when we surrender them to the larger story of God's love. Quite simply, when we surrender to God's love story, our pain and problems can become more about love than about hurt.

The Deepest Story

The way of surrender begins with a commitment to look for love in every story. Whether your story features a sick husband, a wayward daughter, or lonely hours spent by yourself, can you believe that love is the theme God intends to bring into and through your story? It takes humility to acknowledge that what doesn't make sense to us might be about love.

Years ago, I complained to a friend about all of the broken and difficult relationships in my life, and he challenged me, "Sharon, I don't think you would recognize love if it walked right in your front door." When I asked what he meant, he encouraged me to read the Love Chapter, 1 Corinthians 13, and to begin looking for the love described there in my relationship with Jesus. My friend reminded me that a living relationship is mutual and that I shouldn't look just for how Jesus loves me but also for how I love him. He concluded by explaining what he really wanted for me.

"Last night, my wife and I attended a large party for a volunteer organization. We eventually found ourselves on opposite sides of the room, talking to different people, but at one moment I caught my wife's eye and knew that she needed me. I excused myself from the conversation and walked over to her and asked her what she needed. She told me that she had begun to get a terrible headache and that we needed to leave. She thanked me for being attentive to her and for following through with what I noticed."

You are the God who sees me.

—Genesis 16:13 NIV

"That's what I want for you, Sharon," my friend continued. "A love relationship that is so intimate that you notice the smallest things that God is doing and that you know he sees you and is impacted by you as well." I began to cry as my friend shared his heart for me, because isn't that the love story we all long for? To be known and to know. To be seen and to see. To be pursued as we pursue.

The Practice of Looking for Love

I knew that my friend was right, that my pain had become the most real thing in my life and eclipsed any vision of true love, but it scared me to do this exercise and really trust that a love relationship with Jesus could make a difference in my human stories of love lost and found. After my friend Elaine (whom I wrote about in chapter 3) told me about doing a very similar exercise during her time of confinement during treatment for cancer, I surrendered! I surrendered to the practice of looking for love. I want to share some of that practice with you, but before I do, we need to consider the full text of the 1 Corinthians 13 love passage, the perfect guide to falling in love again. Take a deep breath and read it slowly, lingering over each line.

> Love never gives up.
> Love cares more for others than for self.
> Love doesn't want what it doesn't have.
> Love doesn't strut,
> Doesn't have a swelled head,
> Doesn't force itself on others,
> Isn't always "me first,"
> Doesn't fly off the handle,
> Doesn't keep score of the sins of others,
> Doesn't revel when others grovel,
> Takes pleasure in the flowering of truth,
> Puts up with anything,
> Trusts God always,
> Always looks for the best,
> Never looks back,
> But keeps going to the end.
> —1 Corinthians 13:4–7

Every time I read this passage, I smile, because right there in the Bible is the description of my Mr. Right! Most of us have read this passage and have heard that this is a picture of God's love for us—a picture of the love of Jesus, the God-man, the ultimate Man. But I wonder how many of us have read this passage and have considered what we can offer to *him*. Without mutuality, there is no relationship. In his grace, God remains loyal to his nature, which is love. I am so glad that nothing I do or don't do changes his love but that my responses to him shape the nature of our relationship.

Maybe you've never thought about your relationship with Jesus as you would a human relationship. Perhaps your only activity in this relationship happened years ago when you faithfully attended Sunday school, carried your Bible to church, and memorized Bible verses to get stars on a chart. Understandably, those childish responses no longer do much for your spiritual life today. Similarly, in human relationships, if we act in an adult romance as we acted in the romances of our childhood, the romance will fizzle pretty quickly. Oh, how I hope and pray that something is sparked in your heart to fall in love, to fall deeply in love, with the Lover of your soul!

If falling in love with Jesus seems too esoteric or is foreign to the ways you have thought about this relationship, go back and read 1 Corinthians 13 again. The qualities listed in this passage are what we all long for. When we believe that God does not long for these things in relationship as well, we turn him into an austere, unflappable God, so that any experience of relationship is up to us. We want, hope, try, ask, and if we're fortunate, we have enough faith to believe God is pleased. No wonder we get tired and frustrated. If we believe that God too wants, hopes, tries, asks, then our stories intersect with his. The words of the apostle John take on new meaning, "First we were loved, now we love" (1 John 4:19).

We are going to consider the three descriptors in 1 Corinthians 13:4: "Love never gives up. Love cares more for others than for self. Love doesn't want what it doesn't have." The give-and-take of our love life with Jesus is intended to be experienced in a mutual relationship. We persevere because we know that he will never give up on us. Our relationship is deepened when we know that he is thrilled at our trust in him even when he does not perform like a "vending-machine God." We want him even when he doesn't give us what we want; that's love. We can love others, even when they are not that lovely, because we know he sees us at our worst and never loves us less. When I love grouchy, complaining, messy, broken people because God loves me when I'm grouchy, complaining, messy, and broken, that is a partnership cemented by love, an intimacy that delights his heart and fills mine. We can be content in the ups and downs of our lives when we get a glimpse of the unfathomable truth that God loves us just as we are—whether we are in a state of

When I grew up, I left those infant ways for good. We don't yet see things clearly. We're squinting in a fog, peering through a mist. But it won't be long before the weather clears and the sun shines bright! We'll see it all then, see it all as clearly as God sees us, knowing him directly just as he know us! But for right now, until that completeness, we have three things to do to lead us toward that consummation: Trust steadily in God, hope unswervingly, love extravagantly. And the best of the three is love.

—1 Corinthians 13:11–13

grace or disgrace. And when I love him just as he is, not as I need him to be or thought he would be, that is love.

Love Never Gives Up

Let's face it, we give up on God a lot. We don't "hear" from him, we collect unanswered prayers, and we feel his absence is often more real than his presence. What allows us to believe that the silence, the unanswered pleas, and his absence is about love? Maybe it's simply acknowledging what he does when we give up on him: *he keeps on loving us.* Or as Peter Hiett (my wonderful pastor, who relentlessly reminds me of God's love) says, "there is absolutely, truly, and forever no catch. For that means God is not like us ... he is absolute love."[1]

Sometimes human stories give us pictures of what we long for, not only in human relationships but ultimately in our relationship with God. One story that illustrates the beauty of never giving up in relationships is the story of Robertson McQuilkin and his wife, Muriel. Robertson resigned as president of Columbia Bible College to care for his ailing wife. Muriel had Alzheimer's, so instead of running a prestigious evangelical college, every day Robertson bathed Muriel, fed Muriel, and clothed Muriel. Although she was literally losing her mind, he did not give up loving her. He tells the story of taking an airplane trip with Muriel and being delayed in the Atlanta airport. Every few minutes, Muriel would ask the same question and he would give the same answers about what they were doing there and when they were going home. Every few minutes, Muriel would set off walking quickly down the terminal and Robertson would follow after her and bring her back to their seats.

Sitting across from them in the terminal was an attractive younger woman. A well-dressed business executive, she was busily working on her laptop computer and occasionally glanced at Robertson and Muriel in their distracting interactions. Once when they returned from an excursion down the walkway, she mumbled something to them without looking up from her work.

"Pardon?" Robertson asked.

"Oh," she said, "I was just asking myself, 'Will I ever find a man to love me like that?'"[2]

Whether we are single, in a good marriage, or in a difficult relationship, our eager hope as well as our patient (or impatient) endurance and our faithful longing compel us to wonder, Will I ever find someone who will love me like that?

When we refuse to look for God's eager hope, his patient endurance, and his faithful longing to find us in the midst of our pain and to love us even when we give up, we harden our hearts and can't receive love. The longing that arises when we consider what we want in human relationships was designed to make us ask, "Will I ever find Someone who will love me?" When we surrender to his love story, we realize that Jesus romances us to himself through this fallen world and through fallen relationships to show us that he is the only one who will never give up. In this relationship that matters the most, we can surrender our battered and weary hearts to the One who is completely trustworthy. He is faithful when we are faithless.

The Enemy wants us to make our disappointments in relationships the premier reference for understanding our relationship with Jesus. Satan wants to take our broken, difficult, disappointing, even abusive relationships and turn them into our reference point so that we think our relationship with God will be broken, difficult, disappointing, and even abusive.

Will you consider praying that you would have the faith to believe that Jesus never gives up—that he watches even while you sleep? He listens to you breathe. He sings over you, "Beautiful one I love. Beautiful one I adore. Beautiful one— my soul must sing."[3] We surrender to love as the theme of our story when we know that Jesus never gives up on us *and* when our response to his love is to never give up on him. As you surrender your heart to his love, never giving up on him no matter how lonely and loveless you feel, you will develop a real relationship that might even make those around you ask, "Will I ever find Someone to love me like that?"

Love Cares More for Others Than for Self

When I believe that God is loving me in the very story-line that seems most painful, I can love others who are in the midst of heart-wrenching times. How we love others is the evidence of how we experience God's love. It has surprised me that ever since I took my friend's challenge to look for love as described in 1 Corinthians 13, I've been more free to love.

One of the greatest joys I've experienced this past year is hosting a group of women in my home once a week. These women all live at Street's Hope, a rescue mission for women who have been trapped in the sex-trade industry. Our time together is never a burden, and it certainly is not just about my ministering to them. It is a natural outpouring of God's care for me in my own desperate circumstances, and it is always an evening of giving and receiving.

It has surprised me that a lot of the gatherings with these broken women have felt like parties. I have never really liked parties. I can't make small talk, I don't have good party clothes, and I never really know what to do with myself when I'm at a party, but I really enjoy partying with the six or seven of us who gather at my home every Thursday night.

Our stories have taken us to some pretty loveless places. We are all addicts. We have engaged in our addictions in some of the best and worst places that you can imagine. Addiction has dragged some of the women into the sex trade at one time in their lives, and it has compelled all of us to "[trade] the glory of God who holds the whole world in his hands for cheap figurines you can buy at any roadside stand" (Rom. 1:23). Some of us have done some shocking sinning, and all of us have sinned in our hearts (where my pastor says is the most damaging place to sin).

We gather around my dining room table, share a meal, and talk about the places where we've been lost and found. We talk about the Twelve Steps and Jesus. This party has no dress code. We take a smoking break halfway through, and we talk honestly about looking for love in all the wrong places. All of us have offered Jesus nothing, and all of us are discovering that he wants to give us everything. That's a reason to party! The New Testament says it this way: "Take a good look, friends, at who you were when you got called into this life. I don't see many of 'the brightest and the best' among you, not many influential, not many from high-society families. Isn't it obvious that God deliberately chose men and women that the culture overlooks and exploits and abuses, chose these 'nobodies' to expose the hollow pretensions of the 'somebodies'? That makes it quite clear.... Everything that we have—right thinking and right living, a clean slate and a fresh start—comes from God by way of Jesus Christ" (1 Cor. 1:26–30).

Surrendering to the love story of God takes us out of our own stories and keeps us from being put off by the stories of others. When only one story matters—his story—we can truly care more for others than for ourselves. When we care most about him, we care best for others.

One Thursday night, we were gathering around the table after the smoking break. We talked about making a fearless and searching inventory of our lives and how we were able to do that because Jesus made a fearless search for us in some of the most unlikely places. We spent some time considering how Jesus really did care more for us than for himself. "He had equal status with God but didn't think so much of himself that he had to cling to the advantages of that status no matter what" (Phil. 2:6). In the middle of our meeting, one of the women closed her eyes and started reciting a poem that she wrote. Sarah is twenty years old, and she's seen a lot of life in those twenty years. She has been hurt and has hurt herself in places that most of us would never go. Sarah told us that some religious people told her that Jesus wouldn't be caught in the places that she went. Sarah has learned that they were wrong. She's discovered that her deepest story is that Jesus descended into her hell to set her free, and that is why she now chooses to party with people who might never be invited to "high society."

> *Whatever you did for one of the least of these . . . you did for me.*
>
> —Matthew 25:40 NIV

Sarah gave me permission to share her poem. I wish you could hear her recite it. She closes her eyes and tilts her head back when she speaks. Her short, spiral curls spring up and fall. Her voice is rich with passion and sorrow, and when she talks—well, it's a party!

> I am shivering on this bus shelter bench
> When I see a girl
> Maybe sixteen
> Clad in a dirty miniskirt
> Shaking like me
> And my offering
> Is only a dollar
> But God takes it
> Smiles at me
> And jumps into the next car
> I lie crying on the floor
> Staring at an empty pot

And my offering today
Is bits of flour mixed with dirt and mud
God takes the cookies
He smiles and laughs
And that little bit makes his hunger go away
Enough for him to sleep in my arms
As fists connect to face and
As he tells me he fell down
A flight of stairs
I know being gay
Cannot save you from domestic violence
And I can't fix this
My offering is a bag of ice
And God takes it grabs it
And brings it up to his face as he cries
God bends over the toilet releasing the contents
Of her stomach for the fifth time today
And I don't know what to do
So my offering is to hold her hair
And wash her face and mouth afterwards
And she thanks me for not judging her
God just witnessed someone shoot at his house
In the dead of night
And he comes out of the house in his pj's
Adorned with heavy artillery
And I live across the street
And instead of staying inside and
Ducking under furniture
I rush out to help him
And my offering is trying to talk
him out of revenge
You see
I never tell people to shut up
'Cuz I see God in their sufferings
I have seen God shoot up and

Held him as he came down
I've seen God run away from an abusive partner
I've held God as she told me about
Being gang-raped at a frat party
God ain't screaming out for offerings
Of millions and money
But of time and community[4]

Does this personalization of God in real-life stories disturb you? When we don't believe that God enters our stories, feels what we feel, uses these experiences to romance us to himself, then we will be inviting others to an impersonal, distant, duty-bound relationship with God. Further, we will offer to hurting, broken people only out of our own experience, not in partnership with a God who feels pain and wants to heal, who longs for relationship and is willing to sacrifice for that relationship, and who has endured hell for us so that he might invite us to resurrection.

Perhaps you don't share Sarah's view of God, but I wonder how you do see God in your story. If he is only an austere, distant, unflappable God, it will be hard to believe that he cares about the realities in your relationships and that you can care for him in tangible ways. This is the give-and-

> *It's obvious, of course, that he didn't go to all this trouble for angels. It was for people like us. . . . That's why he had to enter into every detail of human life. Then, when he came before God as high priest to get rid of the people's sins, he would have already experienced it all himself— all the pain, all the testing— and would be able to help where help was needed.*
>
> —Hebrews 2:16–18

take of the greatest love story every told. We can care for others only to the degree that we know, heart and soul, that God enters our real-life stories and cares for us with tender love. We can care for him only to the degree that we care for others more than we care for ourselves. As I meet with the women from Street's Hope, I am discovering that the greatest love story is the one that is written as Jesus and I care for others with an abandon that keeps me from looking at only myself.

Love Doesn't Focus on What It Doesn't Have

There's nothing like thinking about our relationships to remind us that we often don't have what we want. We are not alone. Jesus entered this world seeking relationships with us, knowing from the beginning that we would fall short. "He didn't, and doesn't, wait for us to get ready. He presented himself for this sacrificial death when we were far too weak and rebellious to do anything to get ourselves ready. And even if we hadn't been so weak, we wouldn't have known what to do anyway. We can understand someone dying for a person worth dying for, and we can understand how someone good and noble could inspire us to selfless sacrifice. But God put his love on the line for us by offering his Son in sacrificial death while we were of no use whatever to him" (Rom. 5:6–8).

When I know that God loves me when I am good for nothing, then I begin to want to love him even when he doesn't deliver exactly what I want. I want him simply because he is good. That is intimacy. If I am truly longing for and lacking the relationships I want most, then I am dependent on him for everything. This poverty becomes a gift of love when it compels me to trust God. Experiencing the love of God in the midst of pain takes all the sting out of being relationally poor. In his embrace, we are rich indeed, for we are loved just as we are. When we submit and surrender our wants to the care of God, he fills our emptiness with love. Truly, we can look into the eyes of our neediness and see Christ himself. To see him during times of need, we have to surrender—to wanting to see him more than wanting everything to work in the way and in the time that we think it should work.

> *By love God can be caught and held, but by thinking never.*
>
> —Anonymous,
> *The Cloud of Unknowing*

A few years ago, I headed off on a trip to speak at a women's retreat in the Midwest. My daughter was sixteen years old at the time. As I hugged her and told her goodbye, she whispered in my ear, "Mom, you are always gone at the most important times in my life. I hope nothing too big happens while you are gone!" My heart sank, and I immediately wanted to defend myself by listing all the times I had been there for her and demanding that she list even one important event that I had missed.

As I was sitting on the airplane fuming about my short-sighted daughter, I began to think about how I react to God. Whenever there is a bump in the road, I am prone to allow that difficulty to characterize the entire journey and to blame God for any discomfort. It takes commitment and practice to be still in the times of hurt or confusion and be content—with God. The psalmist wrote, "When I get really afraid I come to you in trust" (Ps. 56:3). God longs for us to come to him in trust when we are afraid, angry, lonely, discouraged. We come to him, but often it is with accusations or demands. My heart sank when my daughter came to me with accusations and threats in the midst of her anxiety about my leaving.

While I was at the retreat, my daughter called me. She explained that her best friend was going through a rough time at home and that she had taken some of her distress out on Kristin. They'd had a terrible fight. I braced myself to hear of yet another significant event that I was missing due to my travels. Then Kristin told me that she had baked some chocolate-chip cookies, made a CD of her favorite songs, and left them in her friend's car in the parking lot of the high school. She also decorated the car with balloons and wrote on the car windows phrases that are most meaningful to teenage girls, like "Amber is hot!" and "Love ya, girl!" After Kristin told me about her kind gesture toward her hurting friend, I said, "Wow! Honey, that's awesome! What made you think of doing all that?" Kristin's response is an answer I still cherish today when I am on the road and feeling distant from my family: "I just thought about what you would tell me to do, Mom."

Kristin's remembrance of me in the midst of difficulty and her reliance on things that had been true in our relationship brought great, great joy to my heart! We cannot underestimate the joy we bring to God's heart when we remember and rely on all that is true of him even, and especially, when we are in distress.

More Than Happily Ever After

When we begin to look for something more real than our pain, we discover the Love that has been looking for us all our lives and that we've been looking for all our lives. The apostle Paul summed up the reality of a commitment to fall in love with Jesus again and again: "I want you woven into a tapestry of love, in touch with everything there is to know of God. Then you will have minds confident and at rest, focused on Christ" (Col. 2:2).

Years ago, I worked as a counselor during a weeklong intensive counseling experience for women who had experienced sexual abuse. One woman that I worked with experienced more pain than I could even imagine. She had been sexually abused by her father. Her husband had divorced her after he had an affair with her best friend. And just eighteen months earlier, her son died from AIDS. Near the end of the week, she told me, "Sharon, there's one more thing that I haven't told anyone." As a young therapist, my mind raced, wondering what terrible reality could be left for this woman to disclose.

With some hesitation and almost in a whisper, she told me her deepest secret, "I don't believe that God loves me." Who could blame her after all that she had suffered? I knew that I didn't have words to comfort her in her intense pain, but I asked her if she would be willing to look for God's love in her life story, and she agreed. Two years later, I received the most amazing letter from this dear woman. With her permission, I quote part of her letter: "I realized that God had not put me here to live happily ever after, but that he wasn't looking down from heaven saying, 'Good, let her suffer.' Forgiveness, grace, mercy, gratitude, compassion—had I expected all of these things to come naturally? I guess I had. I am beginning to believe—in the midst of my brokenness—that God has been looking down from heaven saying, 'Good, she's learning to love.' I am discovering that all of this relational pain has not been just about love. The very relational struggles themselves have been love."

Wherever you find yourself in your own story today, I pray you will come to believe that yours is a story about Love. Surrender to the Story.

Just for You

1. Have you ever determined that you would never allow yourself to be hurt again? How did making this vow affect you and your relationships?

2. Think about a difficult story in your relational life. Can you see

ways that God used this painful experience to demonstrate his love for you?

3. How have you experienced God's faithfulness to you? How are you faithful to him?

4. How has pain in your relationships allowed you to care for others in pain? How has it allowed you to care for God?

5. When God does not "deliver" what you want in relationships, how does that affect your relationship with him?

6. What keeps you from surrendering to the belief that the Story behind your story is one of love?

Believe Again

Would you know the Lord's meaning in this? Learn it
well. Love was the meaning. Who showed it to you?
Love. What did he show you? Love. Why did he show
you? For love.

—Julian of Norwich,
All Shall Be Well

WHEN MY DAUGHTER WAS five years old, she determined
that she was going to learn to ride her bicycle without train-
ing wheels, but she quickly discovered that it didn't come
naturally to her. We spent a few afternoons with my running
after her, letting go, only to rush toward her as she crashed on
the sidewalk. After one particularly hard fall, Kristin cried in
anguish, "Mom, I didn't know anything could be this hard!"
The next morning, I awoke to hear my determined daughter
going out the front door. I watched as she took her pink two-
wheeler and began to try to find the right balance to ride it herself. For hours she went up and down the sidewalk in front of
our house. I eventually got busy with other responsibilities and
forgot about my braveheart daughter's quest to ride her bike.

Several hours later, she rushed into the kitchen with a look of triumph on her face. "Come watch me, Mom!" she nearly shouted with joy. I went to the front yard and watched as she balanced herself on her bike and rode up and down the sidewalk. When she finished her display, she got off her bike and ran to hug me. "Oh, honey, I'm so proud of you," I said. I will never forget her reply. "Mom, if you would have told me that it would take just 421 tries, I wouldn't have been so discouraged yesterday!"

Perhaps the most important word in the title of this book and in the title of this chapter is *again*. Relationships become the context in which, at one time or another, we all inevitably exclaim, "I didn't know anything could be this hard!" We become the lovers that God intended us to be when we are willing to try again, risk again, hope again, begin again, and believe again. I am coming to believe that this word *again* is probably one of the most important and most difficult words to live out. Whether it's beginning a diet again, a relationship again, sobriety again, a letter to a long-lost friend again, an apology again, or time with Jesus again—living in "again" is humbling, challenging, and absolutely necessary if we are to become the women we long to be and God intended us to be.

We have considered the realities of difficult and heartbreaking relationships and the ways that Jesus longs to draw us to himself again and again in the midst of our pain and confusion. When we finally surrender to knowing him, wanting him, and loving him—no matter what is going on in our relational lives—we discover the deepest longing of our hearts. I imagine the day when we will stand before the One who loves us most and proclaim, "If you had told me that it would take only beginning again and believing again to have this relationship with you, I wouldn't have been so discouraged."

In his wonderful book, *A Taste of Silence*, Carl Arico writes,

"Transformation is the process of God's recreating our very selves.... All the phases of transformation are not done through our strategies. They are done to us because we are open to remaining in the presence of God."[1] I hope it will be encouraging to spend a little time looking at what we need to believe again to remain open to the presence of God. Relational difficulties either can shut us down and close our hearts or they can become the context for radical transformation, if we are open enough to believe again — in suffering, in surrender, in a Savior, and in surprise!

Believe Again in Suffering

I will turn fifty years old in a few weeks, and it feels like I should by now have a PhD in human suffering. I have been privileged to hear a lot of stories of pain and suffering and to experience a few of them myself. We cannot be afraid of suffering. Most of the woundedness and confusion that we inflict on others and ourselves comes from running from pain. The only thing worse than feeling pain is not feeling it. But we need to keep our eyes on the prize: experiencing the love of God in our life stories. That's difficult to do when we believe that the prize is relationships that always work.

Once when Kristin was four years old, she was running around in the foyer with other children after church. As their game of tag became increasingly wild, she ran headlong into a brick wall, planting her face right into the hard surface. Blood gushed from her mouth as I picked her up and raced her to the emergency room. Her little body shook as she lay on the bed and the doctor gently examined her face. As tears flowed from her eyes, she looked directly into my eyes. When the doctors and nurses bent over her, she craned her neck around them so that she would not lose sight of me. Her terrified eyes spoke for her, "Mom, am I going to be okay?"

This emergency room scene reminds me that when I gave my children presents, their eyes would immediately focus on the surprise packages. I could almost see their brains working to guess what might be in the brightly wrapped presents. When I gave them rules, their eyes darted everywhere above, below, and around me. I often had to get their attention to change their behaviors by sternly saying, "Look at me!" But whenever my children suffered, their eyes always rested on me. Even as young adults, when they are in trouble or hurting, they will call me, and I imagine their plaintive eyes searching for my face, wondering, "Mom, am I going to be okay?"

God allows us to experience suffering in the most precious and painful of contexts—our relationships—in the hope that the suffering will draw our eyes to him. He longs for us to ask, "Father, am I going to be okay?" so that he can gently remind us that he sees us, he hears us, and he understands us. As we believe in the transformative power of suffering, we grow from angry and fearful women whose eyes are on our human relationships, to women resting and full of faith with our eyes on the relationship that sustains us. As King George VI said in his famous 1940 radio talk, "Go out into the darkness, and put your hand into the Hand of God. That shall be better than light, and safer than a known way."

Believe Again in Surrender

We will not experience the transformative power of suffering if we don't surrender. Surrender affects our manner of being in the world rather than our manner of doing. Surrender allows me to tell the truth about my life—nothing more, nothing less. Surrender allows us to be a gentle presence to ourselves, to others, and to God. Surrender frees us from embarrassment about our difficulties in relationships. In fact, surrender allows us to stop spending so much energy trying to get everyone else to change, because we long most for our own transformation.

The reason we have to be reminded to believe in the life-changing power of surrender again and again is because surrender is scary. For many of us who have been hurt in relationships, trying to remain in control seems like the only option left. But surrender requires that we look directly and honestly at our most painful, wonderful, or confusing relationships and ask God what he wants to reveal about us and our relationship with him. That can be terrifying. We can't control him.

I got a living reminder of this truth several months ago when I had dinner with friends who have three small children. I arrived a little early and witnessed the all-too-familiar chaos that circles around a mom of young children as she tries to accomplish anything. I invited the three kids to play a game so that Mom could put her finishing touches on the dinner.

The kids wanted to play Sardines. They explained to me that Sardines is a game of hide-and-seek in which one person hides and then as they are found by others in the game, the others hide with them until everyone is found by the remaining person. Eight-year-old Amelia offered to hide. We counted to one hundred while she found her hiding place. Her six-year-old sister, Annie, was the first to find her. I found Amelia and Annie hiding in an empty cupboard in the corner of their dark, unfinished basement. We crowded together and waited for their four-year-old brother, Andy, to find us. We poked one another, giggled, and *sssshhhh*ed each other as we waited for Andy.

About five minutes passed before we heard Andy walking down the basement stairs. We heard him talking to himself with his shaky four-year-old voice, "I not afraid. I not afraid of the dark." My sympathetic heart wanted to call out to Andy,

"It's okay. We're all down here," but I knew his sisters would never forgive me for giving away our hiding place. When Andy finally opened the cupboard door, we all jumped out at him and starting hugging him. Amidst peals of laughter, Andy exclaimed, "Everything I'm looking for is right here!"

Sometimes we need to face our deepest fears to find all that we are longing for. In all of the twists and turns of our human relationships, God remains steadfast to his deepest longing: to be in an intimate relationship with us. He will use our children, our marriages, our friendships, our loneliness, our joy, our sorrow, and our fears to uncover our deepest longing: to be in an intimate relationship with him. Surrender to him is what we were made for. It is the original intention of our design for relationships. Surrender is not just a lofty thought or an inspiring idea; it is the way in which we may know him. Quite simply, surrender allows us to say, "It may take 421 tries, but beginning again and believing again is worth it, because I am discovering a relationship that is my heart's true desire."

Believe Again in Stories

This past year, one of my dear friends snuck into my purse when I wasn't looking. She made a copy of my house key because she was worried about me. She knew that I was working too many hours, traveling a lot, and experiencing some pain in significant relationships. She took the key "just in case"—just in case I didn't answer my phone or didn't return emails; just in case I hid when she knew what I needed most was community. One morning I awoke to hear voices in my living room. I pulled on my robe and walked downstairs to find five people from my church community waiting for me! To be honest, I was a little mad. I at least wanted to shower and put on a little lipstick before I showed others the brokenness in my life.

My friends asked good questions, prayed for me, and told me that they weren't going anywhere. At first, I felt a bit like a deer caught in the headlights, but gradually, as my friends would not let me hide the painful truths about my life, I began to feel the freedom of living in the light. Over the next month, friends from my church community came to see me every day. They brought me flowers and cookies. They prayed for me. They ate meals with me. At the end of the month, my friend who had snooped through my purse had a party for me. All of my friends came, and we all talked about our difficulties in relationships, our sometimes destructive coping strategies, and our hope in being honest with each other. My pastor says it well: when we hide in community, it should feel like trying to hide under a bikini made of fig leaves in the middle of a hurricane!

Two amazing things have resulted from telling the truth about my life. First, I have experienced more joy than I thought possible. I believe more than ever Jesus' statement that "the truth will free you" (John 8:32). Second, my friends are much freer to tell the truth about their stories. They didn't want to snoop and judge me; they wanted to be a part of my story, and they wanted me to be a part of their stories as well. Emotional healing takes place only in community, as we tell our stories again and again.

I have told the stories of many remarkable women in the pages of this book. You many find helpful encouragement in an update on some of their stories.

Annie, the woman who discovered her "kinsman-redeemer" in Matt, has another baby. She and her sweet family live in a southern state, where Annie works in a hospital in the addictions unit. She has sent me many emails telling me about the opportunities she has to sit alongside broken, desperate people and tell them that she *knows* they too can begin again.

Liza, the beautiful mother of adopted baby Selah, recently wrote me about a terrifying night when Selah became very ill and they had to rush her to the hospital. She is grateful that Selah survived her illness, but the work required to care for her often leaves Liza exhausted. Liza had put her dreams of returning to graduate school on hold to care for Selah, but she is now beginning to explore the possibilities of going back to school if they can find help with the care and support that Selah needs. My heart aches for Liza because she has experienced so many shattered dreams, but my heart is also convicted and challenged by Liza's response. She surrendered to her story, believing that it is a part of a deeper story, and she and her husband, Sam, are making plans to travel to Ethiopia to adopt another baby. Her faith to begin again, risk again, and believe again reminds me that our stories are intended to land us not in a place of "happily ever after" but in a place where we "trust steadily in God, hope unswervingly, [and] love extravagantly" (1 Cor. 13:13).

Elaine, my friend with the wedding dress hanging on the back of her bedroom door, has completed the recommended treatment for her thyroid cancer. The doctors believe that the treatment has been successful. Sometimes Elaine is anxious and wonders what suffering will come next, but more often she is resting. She often invites friends over to share a meal and sometime invites herself over to spend the night at their houses, because she has learned that sharing sorrow and joy, faith and anxiety, results in rich relationships. In fact, Elaine is the friend who stole the key out of my purse to "force" me into community. She knows it is not good for us to be alone!

Kristin, my dear daughter who has given me stories of great joy and sorrow, is now a married woman! Her brother, Graham, gave a wonderfully meaningful toast at her rehearsal dinner. He reminded her of how they used to play "wedding" when they were little. Kristin told Graham what to wear, how to walk, and what to say in their ceremonies. Graham reminded Kristin of one of the home videos, which we have watched over and over again, of my toddler children playing their game of wedding. In the video, Graham is about two years old, and his gait is a little shaky. Kristin is leading (dragging) him down her make-believe aisle, which is in our living room and passes by an open stairwell into the basement. The camera shows their approach to the stairs, and then almost as if on cue, as they walk by the stairs, Graham topples over and falls down the steps. The picture blurs as the cameraman drops the camera to rescue Graham, but you can hear Kristin yelling, "Graham, get back up here! We're not through!"

In his toast, Graham told his sister that she has always gone before him. He has watched her struggle with her faith, face her alcoholism, work hard for sobriety, and then offer her experience, strength, and hope to so many others. He concluded by saying, "Thank you for always being someone I want to follow!" His toast and the story he told would not be as meaningful without all of the ups and downs (some literal!). The Grand Storyteller of our lives is committed to making us into women whom others can follow straight into his story!

Sally, the friend I met in Alcoholics Anonymous who also introduced me to the Twelve Step meeting in jail, recently checked into the jail to serve a six-month sentence for her DUI conviction. I imagine she was scared, but I know she is filled with a peace beyond all human understanding. A few days before she went in, she explained to me, "Sharon, I fell on my knees on the concrete outside the courthouse before my sentencing. I surrendered my story to Jesus. It's not mine anymore. I made a mess of it anyway. It's his." Sally doesn't even know this yet, but her story is already impacting others. Yesterday I received a phone call from a client of mine who has been struggling with her sobriety. She has been in and out of treatment and has had a hard time surrendering. She called and left a message saying, "Sharon, I'm ready to surrender. There was a woman at our meeting whose name is Sally who is going to jail, and I have never seen such peace in my life. I want what she has!"

I know that what Sally "has" is not a program or even mastered steps toward better living. Sally is surrendered to Jesus, and that has made all the difference.

Believe Again in a Savior

One of my favorite quotations about marriage and our confusion about the purpose of relationships is from Gina Bria: "We all marry the wrong person. We marry the person we end up wanting to kill, cut up into little pieces, and hide in the freezer. That's because we all marry for salvation love, and salvation never comes from the side. It only comes from above."[2] All suffering in relationships was intended to remind us that we cannot save ourselves or each other. We need a Savior.

My friend Dottie, the woman from whom I took front-porch lessons in hope, recently lost her battle with ovarian cancer. A few days after I sat on her bedside and massaged her back, a hospice nurse told me that Dottie didn't have much time left. I could tell that this world with all of its difficulties and disappointments in relationships was fading for Dottie. Another world and another relationship were becoming more real. Dottie slept a lot near the end of her life, but there was a moment when she grabbed my hand and seemed to be fully awake. "Sharon," she whispered, "there is only Jesus." I knew that for Dottie, the shadows of this world had been eclipsed by the substance of her faith: Jesus. Her story had been swallowed up by a deeper story. When we surrender to a Savior, we find that he not only answers our deepest needs but also empowers us to respond to the needs of others.

Jesus, the Answer to Our Needs

When we believe that relationships are the answer to the longings of our hearts, we can become consumed with shaping relationships to meet our needs. We spend a lot of time describing our needs to others, discovering our love language and the love language of others, so that all our needs can be met—only to end up discouraged and frustrated because we're still needy. Our needs are important. As we acknowledge them to ourselves and to others, they can become the context for vulnerable communication, sacrificial giving, and delightful receiving. But no husband, friend, or child out there is enough to meet all of our needs. Needs are important primarily because they reveal how far short any human being comes in satisfying our needs.

One of Jesus' most intriguing statements in the New Testament is, "Anyone who comes to me but refuses to let go of father, mother, spouse, children, brothers, sisters—yes, even one's own self!—can't be my disciple" (Luke 14:26). Notice that Jesus didn't say that the proof of discipleship is a relational life—with father, mother, spouse, children, brothers, and sisters—that meets all of our needs. When we hide in shame because of difficulties in relationships, we miss the opportunity that these difficulties were intended to give us. An intimate relationship with Jesus is not possible without the painful realities of loneliness and heartache. Without tasting these experiences, we cannot be fully Christlike. Heartache and failure in relationships reveal our need of him and provide an opportunity for us to become more like him, as we participate together in the fellowship of suffering. "The *via dolorosa*, the path to the cross, must be trod alone. Like the dock before the very judgment-seat of God, this is a narrow place, wide enough for only one abreast. There is no marriage in heaven, taught Jesus (see Matt. 22:30). We squeak through the pearly gates one by one."[3]

I am convinced that one of the most costly mistakes we make is holding up relationships that work as the pinnacle of growth and maturity. This is costly, first of all, because we may stay in a state of tormented discontent if we believe that good relationships are ones in which we get all of our needs met. We become demanding of others and disappointed in them when they can't meet all of our needs. But there is another cost as well. We may give up on anyone not fully meeting our needs and determine that we need to find the formula that allows us to compensate for the failures of others, take care of our own needs, and not feel the continued longing for relationships. We believe that our neediness must be either constantly soothed by others or denied, hidden, or numbed by ourselves. I think that we buy a lot of self-help books to find a way to make our neediness—the beautiful ache—go away.

Our needs—our longings for relationships and the ache that remains for more even when we experience good relationships—are not intended to lead us in a mad pursuit to make our marriages wonderful, our children compliant, and our friendships always abundant. If that's all that you long for, you'll never be able to rest. Those great relationships can be challenged, changed, or even ripped away at a moment's notice, plunging you into despair about your neediness again. Our needs were intended to remain in good, bad, daily, and difficult relationships, because the hallmark of growth and maturity is wanting a relationship with our Savior more than we want anything else. That requires humility, surrender, and a commitment to a constant relationship with him in the midst of our neediness, because even Jesus doesn't meet all of our needs. He is the answer that wants to be investigated for eternity!

Jesus, the Answer to the Needs of Others

Our stories are redeemed by the deeper story of our Savior's love when we realize that our pain gives us something to offer to the world. He saves us, not to be stuck in ourselves or even to offer ourselves to others, but to offer him to others.

Author and theologian Francis MacNutt writes about a man named Michael Gaydos, who, after the healing of his impaired eyesight, has been effective in a ministry of healing prayer for those with similar afflictions. MacNutt writes, "His experience leads us to an interesting conclusion: people who have been healed of a particular ailment seem to have a special gift from that point on in ministering to people with the same problem. Perhaps it is because they now have greater faith in the area in which they themselves have directly experienced God's power."[4] Your struggles in relationships and how those struggles have pointed you toward the healing path are what you have to offer to other struggling people.

As we experience the Savior's presence with us in the midst of our failures, we learn how to be with others in the midst of their failures. One of the most telling questions for what you believe about your story is, Do you react to the needs of others, or do you respond to their needs as an opportunity to experience God's redemptive presence? Reacting would be scrambling to take care of their needs and keep them from being uncomfortable. We are reacting when we diminish people's needs and say things like, "Oh, it's not that bad. Others have suffered far worse," or, "God will work everything out if you just trust him." We are reacting when the needs of others so overwhelm us that we distance ourselves from messy people. We are responding to the needs of others when we know, heart and soul, that in our own stories, neediness has been the place where we have most powerfully experienced God's redemptive presence. We are responding when we can listen to the pain, anger, and confusion of others without judging them. We are responding when we don't require others to "get it all together" in order to be in relationship with us. We are responding when we can sit in the dark with others in need, confident that the Light is just ahead.

Believe Again in Surprise

When we surrender our suffering to the Savior, we are surprised to discover the Love we've been looking for all of our lives. One of my favorite Bible stories is the one Jesus tells about the person who sells everything he owns to buy a field that contains a treasure. It's important to note that the field itself is not the treasure; the treasure is buried in the field, and Jesus notes that the treasure is only "accidentally found" (Matt. 13:44) by the person who then buys the field. Maybe you've read this story and wondered what it has to do with you. You may not think a lot about real estate, but I suspect you think about relationships, and relationships are the "field" where we find the greatest treasure. You are in the right place to discover this treasure

- when you are struggling with depression, loneliness, and shame because of difficult or broken relationships and honestly confess your struggles.
- when you have experienced brokenness and hurt in your family of origin but are open to risking again in new relationships.
- when you no longer let pain keep you locked in, but you move out toward others who may be hurting too.
- when you offer to others the gifts of wisdom and encour-

agement, from the depths of your own painful experiences.

- when you want to trust again more than you want to protect yourself from being hurt.
- when you want to hope again more than you want the illusion of security that comes with being in control.
- when you want to fall in love again in an intimate relationship with Jesus more than you want all of the other human relationships you have dreamed about and have worked so hard for.

Regardless of where you are in your story, you will miss the surprise treasure if you just become a really good actress and pretend that all is well in your relational life. That's what we do in our culture; we play it safe, take care of ourselves, look out for number one, do all things in moderation, and so on. Because the truth seems a little foolish, we pour our hearts and souls into relationships with no guarantee of the outcome, and we encourage one another to live the lie that everything is working. We long for these relationships more than anything else. We were created for them. And then they don't work. We sell all that we have to buy the field, and it may seem like a big waste if we don't know that the field isn't the treasure; the treasure is buried in the field. Relationships aren't the treasure, but they contain all that we need to find the true treasure. I suspect that God may even lead us to difficult relationships so that he can lead us through them to Jesus.

God Loves Foolish Women

I am glad women are willing to look like fools for relationships. It was the women who went to the tomb of the crucified Jesus and then reported to everyone they met that Jesus was no longer dead (see Luke 24:9–11). Everyone thought they were telling idle tales, that they were fools—until Jesus showed up. To believe again is to be a fool. It is to finally answer the One who unashamedly and foolishly proclaims, "Look at me. I stand at the door. I knock. If you hear me call and open the door, I'll come right in and sit down to supper with you" (Rev. 3:20).

This intimate relationship with Jesus is for fools, not because it's untrue but because this whole world is untrue, and nothing proves that more than our difficulties in relationships. Yet those very difficulties are what can compel us to want Jesus more than we want any human relationship. When we ignore his knocking at our door in the midst of painful or difficult relationships, we build dungeons for our souls. When we don't realize that relational realities are intended to compel us to hear his knocking, we miss the Truth and we miss being discovered by the Truth.

Who is willing to be a fool—again and again? Usually it is the outcasts, the unchosen, the broken, the disenfranchised; those who have learned not to put their faith in the "field"—the relationships of the world—but to risk all that they have in that field for the hope of finding the treasure. The New Testament expresses it this way, "God chose the foolish things of this world [risking in relationships again] to shame the wise [playing it safe]; God chose the weak things of the world [brokenness in relationships] to shame the strong [looking like we have it all together]. He chose the lowly things of this world [difficult relationships] and the despised things [failed relationships]—and the things that are not [loneliness] ... so that no one may boast before him. [That Christ Jesus might] become for us wisdom from God—that is, our righteousness, holiness and redemption" (1 Cor. 1:27–30 NIV).

In revealing his desire for a relationship with us, God chooses foolishness—broken, painful, confusing, heartbreaking, human relationships. When you are in the midst of a relationship that is not working, remember that a treasure is buried in that field. When you are in a fulfilling, good relationship, don't make the mistake of believing that it's the treasure. Believe again that the grand surprise of God is found in the "field" of human relationships: the treasure of an intimate relationship with Jesus!

The best benediction I know for those who would love with abandon and sell all that they have to begin again and believe again that the treasure in the midst of all the human relationships is knowing Jesus more intimately comes from the pen of the apostle Paul: "So this is my prayer: that your love will flourish and that you will not only love much but well. . . . Live a lover's life, circumspect and exemplary, a life Jesus will be proud of: bountiful in fruits from the soul, making Jesus Christ attractive to all, getting everyone involved in the glory and praise of God" (Phil. 1:9–11).

May you know that you are loved. May you love because you have been loved. And in loving, may you know intimately the One who is the beginning and ending of all of our stories.

Notes

Introduction

1. A "kinsman-redeemer" is an Old Testament reference to someone who is "next of kin" who "buys back, avenges, delivers, redeems, and rescues." *The Oxford Desk Dictionary and Thesaurus* (NY: Berkley Books, 1997).

Chapter One: The Beautiful Ache

1. Daniel Clendenin, "The Parallel Universe of the Passion of Jesus," (Palo Alto, Calif.: JourneywithJesus.net), March 16, 2008.

2. Carol Lee Flinders, *At the Root of this Longing* (San Francisco: HarperCollins, 1998), 20.

3. Used by permission. Anonymous ("Liza"), "Reflections on the Addiction Class" (Orlando, Fla.: Reformed Theological Seminary, July 2008), 1.

4. Ibid.

5. Alexander Roberts and James Donaldson, eds., *The Writings of Origen*, trans. Frederick Crombie, (Chestnut Hill, Mass.: Adamant Media, 2001), 241.

6. "Reflections on the Addiction Class," 1.

Chapter Two: The Gift of Brokenness

1. Henri J. M. Nouwen, *In the Name of Jesus* (NY: Crossroad, 1989), 53.

2. David G. Benner, *The Gift of Being Yourself* (Downers Grove, Ill.: InterVarsity Press, 2004), 54.

Chapter Three: The Hope of Strange Women

1. Referenced in Dana Crawley Jack, *Silencing the Self* (NY: HarperCollins, 1991), 89.

2. Mary Pipher, *The Shelter of Each Other* (NY: Grosset/Putnam, 1996), 117.

3. Richard Rohr, *Simplicity: The Freedom of Letting Go* (NY: Crossroad, 1990), 57.

4. Ibid.

5. Robert Farrar Capon, *Kingdom, Grace, Judgment: Paradox, Outrage, and Vindication in the Parables* (Grand Rapids, Mich.: Eerdmans, 2002), 300.

6. Tessa Bielecki, *Teresa of Avila* (London: Shambhala, 1996), 11.

Chapter Four: The Valley of Humiliation

1. Janet Fitch, *White Oleander* (Boston: Little, Brown, 1999), 403.

2. Rachel Stratford. Used by permission.

3. Dan Allender, *To Be Told* (Colorado Springs, Colo.: WaterBrook, 2005), 181.

Chapter Five: The Desert of Estrangement

1. Gene Edwards, *Exquisite Agony* (Jacksonville, Fla.; SeedSowers, 2004), 13.

2. Ibid., 17.

3. Ibid., 19.

4. Ibid., 61.

5. Ibid., 88.

6. Yehudit Inbar, from an interview in *Spots of Light: To Be a Woman in the Holocaust*, Yad Vashem Holocaust Museum, Jerusalem, 2006.

7. Richard Rohr, *Simplicity* (NY: Crossroad, 1990), 80.

8. Peter Hiett, "Faith for Cursing Fig Trees" (sermon, Lookout Mountain Community Church, Golden, Colo., February 13, 2005).

9. Dan Allender, *Mars Hill Newsletter*, April 29, 2009.

10. Edwards, *Exquisite Agony*, 91.

Chapter Six: The Fruit of Loneliness

1. Henri J. M. Nouwen, *The Inner Voice of Love* (NY: Doubleday, 1996), 117, italics added.

2. Stephen R. Covey, *Principle-Centered Leadership* (NY: Simon and Schuster, 1992), 161.

3. Brennan Manning, *The Signature of Jesus* (Sisters, Oreg.: Multnomah, 1988), 214.

Chapter Seven: Daring to Trust Again

1. Norman Cousins, *Head First: The Biology of Hope and the Healing Power of the Human Spirit* (NY: Penguin, 1990), 211.

2. Brennan Manning, *Ruthless Trust* (San Francisco: HarperCollins, 2000), 8.

3. Ibid.

4. Mike Mason, *The Gospel according to Job* (Wheaton, IL: Crossway, 1994), 42.

5. F. B. Meyer, italics added.

Chapter Eight: Living in Hope Again

1. Pearl S. Buck, *To My Daughters, with Love* (NY: Buccaneer, 1992), 87.

2. Alcoholics Anonymous, *Big Book: The Story of How Many Thousands of Men and Women Have Recovered from Alcoholism*, 3rd. ed. (New York: Alcoholics Anonymous World Services, 1976), 449.

3. Ibid.

4. Quoted by Martha Manning in *Chasing Grace* (NY: HarperCollins, 1996), viiii.

5. George MacDonald, *The Seaboard Parish* (Charleston, S.C.: BiblioLife, 2008), 220.

Chapter Nine: Falling in Love Again

1. Peter Hiett, "Why Jesus Rose from the Dead" (sermon, Lookout Mountain Community Church, Golden, Colo., May 2, 2004).

2. Robertson McQuilkin, *A Promise Kept* (Carol Stream, Ill.: Tyndale House, 1998), 68.

3. Jeremy Camp, "Beautiful One" (Seattle: Bec Recordings/Emd, 2004).

4. Sarah Francois. Used by permission.

Conclusion

1. Carl J. Arico, *A Taste of Silence: A Guide to the Fundamentals of Contemplative Prayer* (NY: Continuum International, 1999), 27–28.

2. Gina Bria, *The Art of Family* (NY: Dell, 1998), 112.

3. Mason, *The Gospel according to Job*, 46.

4. As told by Brennan Manning, *The Wisdom of Tenderness* (San Francisco: HarperSanFrancisco, 2002), 49.

Begin Again, Believe Again

Embracing the Courage to Love with Abandon

Sharon A. Hersh,
Author of *Bravehearts*

Embracing the Courage to Love with Abandon

BEGIN
AGAIN,
BELIEVE
AGAIN

Sharon A. Hersh
Author of *Bravehearts*

This audio book tells the stories of women who look for relationships but find failure, brokenness, fractured families, addiction, abuse, judgment, and shattered dreams, and yet somehow muster the courage to get up the next day and still want family, friends, partnerships, healing, and a hope that makes a difference in the lives of individuals and communities. By telling real stories of women who entered young adulthood with brave dreams of creating family, friends, and a purpose in life, and then found things falling apart, this book offers encouraging advice for difficult times. This book reminds us that faith, purpose, strong values, and fierce convictions do not slay the dragons of danger and destruction in our world. In fact a braveheart is not someone who slays a dragon at all. (We only think we should, and can, do that when we are young.) This book encourages women to wake up every morning to begin again, believe again, forgive again, and dwell in the possibilities again—that's what takes a real hero. A braveheart.

Available in stores and online!

ZONDERVAN®
.com

Mothering without Guilt

You and God, You and Others, You and Your Kids

Jean E. Syswerda, General Editor
Written by Sharon Hersh

A Bible-study series addressing the unique needs of moms

These eight Bible studies help women discover God's wisdom on how to be the best mothers, women, and disciples they can be. Each study contains six sessions divided into five flexible portions: For You Alone, For You and God's Word, For You and Others, For You and God, and For You and Your Kids. The last section helps moms share each week's nugget of truth with their children.

Mothering without Guilt identifies and debunks the "perfect mom" stereotypes and encourages moms to be real, not perfect, and forgiven, not guilty.

Share Your Thoughts

With the Author: Your comments will be forwarded to the author when you send them to *zauthor@zondervan.com*.

With Zondervan: Submit your review of this book by writing to *zreview@zondervan.com*.

Free Online Resources at
www.zondervan.com

Zondervan AuthorTracker: Be notified whenever your favorite authors publish new books, go on tour, or post an update about what's happening in their lives at www.zondervan.com/authortracker.

Daily Bible Verses and Devotions: Enrich your life with daily Bible verses or devotions that help you start every morning focused on God. Visit www.zondervan.com/newsletters.

Free Email Publications: Sign up for newsletters on Christian living, academic resources, church ministry, fiction, children's resources, and more. Visit www.zondervan.com/newsletters.

Zondervan Bible Search: Find and compare Bible passages in a variety of translations at www.zondervanbiblesearch.com.

Other Benefits: Register yourself to receive online benefits like coupons and special offers, or to participate in research.

ZONDERVAN.com/
AUTHORTRACKER
follow your favorite authors